NATHALIE DUPREE COOKS

EVERYDAY MEALS FROM A WELL-STOCKED PANTRY

NATHALIE DUPREE COOKS

EVERYDAY MEALS FROM A WELL-STOCKED PANTRY

Strategies for Shopping Less and Eating Better

CLARKSON POTTER/PUBLISHERS

NEW YORK

**I DEDICATE THIS BOOK TO PAM KRAUSS, MY
EDITOR, WHO HAS WORKED SO DILIGENTLY ON THIS
BOOK AND WHO HAS BEEN SUCH A GREAT SUPPORT
THROUGHOUT THE CREATIVE PROCESS.**

Published by Clarkson N. Potter Inc., 201 East 50th Street, New York, New York 10022. Member of the Crown Publishing Group.

Random House, Inc. New York, Toronto, London, Sydney, Auckland

CLARKSON N. POTTER, POTTER, and colophon are trademarks of Clarkson N. Potter, Inc.

Manufactured in the United States of America

Design by Elizabeth Van Itallie

Library of Congress Cataloging-in-Publication Data
Dupree, Nathalie.
    Nathalie Dupree cooks everyday meals from a well-stocked pantry : strategies for shopping less and eating better / by Nathalie Dupree.
        p.   cm.
    Includes bibliographical references and index.
    1. Cookery, American.   I. Title.
TX715.D923   1995
641.5973—dc20   94-31426
                                                       CIP

ISBN 0-517-59735-7
10   9   8   7   6   5   4   3   2

ACKNOWLEDGMENTS

I could not have completed this book without the inspiration and perspiration of the following people: Laura Bradley, Kay Calvert, Bernard Clayton, Sam Collins, Rodney Farmer, Steve Farmer, Bert Greene, Grandmother Kreiser, Ric Lands, Karen Lee, Mère Titine, Jane Mullin, Marjorie Nunn, Amanda Brown Olmstead, Ray Overton, Marianna Reed, Julie Sahni, Patti Scott, Margaret Ann Surber, David Sylvain, Pierre-Henri Thiault, Lu Len Walker, Savannah Walker, Virginia Willis, the Duchess of Windsor, Sally Young, and Dr. Bob Young.

A special thank you goes to Anne Tamsberg, who helped test many of these recipes as my apprentice and who is now an assistant to my editor.

And I can't forget my TV crew: Ric Lands, the culinary producer, and Virginia Willis, the kitchen director, and her crew, who made the food possible—Evan Bernstein, Carol Ritchie, Nancy Maupin, Andrew H. Messerlian, Nancy Muysson, John Peterson, Pat Royalty, Lee Anne Saye, Jennifer Pendleton Stewart, Philip Austin Vogel, Carolyn Williams, and Sally Young, along with Connie Ward-Cameron, my supervising producer, and her production team—Vivian Baker, Phillip Butler, Clement O. McIntosh II, William Kimberly III, C. Rudolph Ingram Jr., Ron Lehr, Boyd Lewis, Tom Lloyd, Mark Miller, Linda Ohmart, Perry Patterson, Robert K. Simmons, Ritch Vogan, and John Williams.

CONTENTS

INTRODUCTION

There was a time when the phrase "pantry meal" connoted something made entirely of nonperishables: pasta with bottled red sauce, tuna casseroles, and three bean salads. Today such meals do little to excite our more sophisticated palates, nor do they reflect our growing appreciation for the pleasures of seasonal fruits and vegetables. However it's only the lucky few who have the luxury of making daily—or even weekly—shopping excursions to search out fresh ingredients. For most of us, everyday cooking means relying on what's in the pantry.

Nowadays, the pantry is more than the old-time pie safe with its tin doors to keep unwanted creatures out, a closet that holds large containers of lard and flour and beans and cornmeal, or a dark basement or root cellar with rickety shelves and jars of put-up beans and preserves dated years back, the ceiling full of hanging things like laundry, Vidalia onions, and hams. The pantry is part of my everyday life and encompasses my freezer, my refrigerator, my kitchen shelves, and even my herb garden. Keeping my pantry replenished and augmenting its contents with the fresh foods I buy on ever more infrequent marketing jaunts are what allow me to put together interesting, varied, and fresh-tasting meals every night without spending hours of my time in the grocery store. In fact, an apt title for this book might have been the *I Hate to Shop More Than Once Every Two Weeks Cookbook*.

It's not that I don't love grocery shopping; I do. But who can stop to smell the melons when there is too much to be done? I've learned it's much more efficient (not to mention economical) to do one massive shop for staples and household necessities like laundry detergent and paper towels once a month or even less, and then supplement those staples with more perishable goods that I buy on weekly or biweekly jaunts. This way I can take advantage of the savings offered by buying paper goods, certain canned items, baking items, and so on and then making less frequent trips to seek out fresh produce, prime meats, and gourmet items.

It takes a while to get a home pantry up to date, and it would cause bankruptcy to purchase everything at once. Use the list on page 13 as your guideline, starting with those items marked with a star—what we call the bomb shelter basics, that core group of indispensable ingredients that, combined in different ways, will ensure you can *always* find *something* to eat in the house—and expand your pantry with additional items from my master list as you go. I keep a list of the routine staples I like to have on hand on the shelves and in cold storage posted on my refrigerator. That way I can note when something is used up and be sure to replace it the next time I shop. This list will vary from family to family—you may consider frozen juice bars or super chunk peanut butter staples if you have kids, or feel you can't face the day without your meusli—but essentially your list should look something like mine.

Throughout the book you'll notice the recipes are marked with symbols indicating which pantry ingredients are required for that particular dish. Those marked 🗍 can be made entirely from the bomb shelter basics, provided you are flexible and savvy about making substitutions. Other recipes are based on these same staples, augmented by additions from one or more of the following categories: 🌶 indicates a recipe that uses fresh ingredients from the vegetable bin or fruit bowl, though in many cases, frozen or canned fruits can be substituted with good results. ⊕ calls for foods from the dairy case, which also encompasses the freezer (for storing things like cream cheese or grated Parmesan) and the kitchen shelf, where you'll be storing powdered milk and canned condensed milk for those times when you're out of fresh (see page 199 for guidelines on buying and storing dairy foods). ⊕ indicates a recipe that derives its appeal from contributions from the international or gourmet pantry, those extravagantly flavored items such as sun-dried tomatoes, dried porcini mushrooms, capers, Greek olives, Mexican chilies, and extra-virgin olive oil that I simply can't cook without these days. The Asian pantry ⊙ is yet another distinctive category, and if you love these flavors as much as I do you'll want to reserve an entire shelf for dark sesame oil, five-spice powder, hoisin sauce, bamboo shoots, and dried Chinese mushrooms. When you see the ⊕ symbol, expect a recipe that relies on contributions from the herb garden and/or spice rack, to lift basics into a savory, full-of-flavor new realm. And ⊕ points out those recipes that will send you to the baking pantry for items like extracts, specialty flours, and so forth; interestingly, these are not restricted to recipes in the baking chapter! See page 166 for tips on what to lay in for a well-stocked baking pantry.

This is absolutely not to suggest that you will want or need to have each and every ingredient on all these lists on hand at all times. Learning to substitute freely and creatively is the essential key to pantry cooking.

If the list of ingredients is long and you are lacking one or two, omit them or substitute. If you don't have goat cheese but do have Monterey Jack, Yogurt Cheese (page 19), or mozzarella, by all means, use it. If you don't have avocado for the salsa, chunk in a ripe peach or peeled cucumber. Ground turkey or chicken can stand in for ground beef, pork loin can substitute for chicken, and so on. Learn to see the odds and ends and leftovers in your refrigerator as raw materials that will add variety and diversity to your menus.

The current style in restaurants of mixing lettuces, fruits, and vegetables has given us new freedom in the home as well and adapts perfectly to this kind of flexible cooking. Use that bit of fresh spinach with the oddments of red leaf lettuce. Jicama is so large you are bound to have leftovers if you buy it for a salad; try it in place of water chestnuts in a stir-fry. Mix broccoli with asparagus if you don't have enough of either to make a side dish.

Here is my basic shopping list, divided into those things that are non-perishable and can be stored on the shelf if unopened, and fresh foods or those requiring refrigeration or freezing. The items marked with a ★ are what we consider bomb shelter basics. If you are sure to have at least one item from each of these starred categories (say, raisins for your dried fruit or a package of frozen shrimp for the fish), you'll be able to make soup, entrée, and a dessert so delicious no one would dream you hadn't a thing in the house when you started cooking.

Nonperishables

*bacon (or vacuum-pack ham or
  sausage)
 baking powder
 baking soda
*broths, stocks, stock concen-
  trate, and canned soups
*canned evaporated and/or
  condensed milk
*canned or dried beans, like
  kidney, garbanzo (chick peas),
  cannelini
*canned vegetables (corn,
  artichokes, beets, potatoes, and
  carrots work best for me)
*chocolate or cocoa powder
 chutneys/relishes/salsa
 coconut
 cornmeal or cornmeal mix
 crackers
*dried fruit (apples, raisins,
  cranberries, currants, cherries,
  figs, prunes, mixed fruits)
*dried mushrooms or duxelles
  (page 101)
 extracts/flavorings
*fish and seafood (anchovies,
  tuna, canned and frozen crab,
  clams, oysters, shrimp)
*flour (all-purpose, wheat, cake)

*herbs and spices, fresh and
  dried,
 jam or jelly
 mayonnaise
*nuts and seeds (walnuts, pine-
  nuts, almonds, pecans, etc.)
 oats, rolled and quick
*oils (vegetable, olive, peanut,
  canola)
*pasta, assorted, including
  couscous
 peanut butter
 pickles/cornichons
*powdered milk and buttermilk
*rice, wild rice, or other grains
  such as quinoa or bulgur
 shortening
 spirits and wines
*sugar (white, brown,
  confectioners')
 sweeteners (maple syrup,
  molasses, honey, corn syrup)
*tomatoes, canned plum,
  wedges, sauce
*vinegars (sherry, cider,
  balsamic, red wine)
 wrappers (wonton skins, crepes,
  tortillas, pitas)
 yeast

Fresh/Frozen Foods

*beef (various cuts) one big cut braise, stew, or roast, plus a pound of ground meat
*butter/margarine (keep a pound in the freezer)
*cheese (one hard cheese, like Parmesan, and one semisoft, like cheddar, cover most needs)
*eggs or frozen egg substitute
*fish (vacuum-packed salmon, crab, oysters, frozen shrimp)

*fruit (whatever your family likes best and keeps well)
*garlic
*heavy cream
*milk
*onions, shallots, red onions
*potatoes
*poultry (a whole chicken and a pound of breast cutlets)
*vegetables including packages of frozen peas, spinach, and/or broccoli for emergencies

No matter how much time you have to shop, you are always better off with a list. That doesn't mean you can't be seduced by the fresh fennel or that a ripe melon won't replace your grapefruit. It just means you should plan out the ratio of fresh to canned or frozen produce to minimize spoilage and keep your cost and your time down—and take advantage of store specials.

Ideally, you will have fresh vegetables to be used over a period of two weeks, with some of them, like beets and cabbage, well able to last for more than that. Similarly, checking the date on your dairy food will enable you to keep it that long as well. And you will have purchased enough dried, canned, and frozen foods for two weeks or even a month. This doesn't mean you won't want to stop at the vegetable stand for some fresh tomatoes. It just means that you will be able to stand in the express lines in the grocery store for the rest of the month as well as reduce the waste of fresh produce to a minimum.

Some other tips might include staggering the ripeness of the fruit you buy. If you are buying ripe peaches, buy green bananas. And rather than buying the three ripe, juicy tomatoes, buy some pale pink and some ripe, letting the pale pink ones ripen in a paper bag for several days until they are a lush red.

Chicken, turkey, and meat may be purchased fresh or frozen. I find it easiest to come home, put a whole chicken on to cook—either poaching it or roasting it—while I am unloading the rest of the groceries. I usually buy one other whole chicken, removing the bag or bags inside, rewrapping it, and freezing it. If I buy chicken breasts, I bone some, adding the bones to the poaching breast to aid in making a wonderful stock and freezing the rest, wrapped, flat on a tray. When frozen, I repack them in a freezer container so I can pull them out one at a time as I need them. I usually divide the ground beef into good-size patties; whether I ultimately use it for burgers or meat loaf, they defrost faster than a frozen pound.

The perfect vegetables to have on hand are those already in their own containers—sweet and regular potatoes, onions, garlic, shallots, zucchini and other squashes, cucumbers, turnips, rutabagas, apples, oranges, bananas, melons, and other fruits. (They can also be put in sacks easily and slipped into spaces in the trunk of the car, much as socks fill up holes in a suitcase.)

I have also learned to save and freeze leftovers, even if only a cup of broth. After all, a cup of broth reheated with some frozen peas and a bit of ginger can make a refreshing pick-me-up.

This does not mean that I lean toward chopped meat extenders or cake mixes, but I do make my own mixes and refrigerator breads. I still like the feeling of putting together my own spices and ingredients, combining the basics. I don't buy frozen meals. I make my own chipped beef on toast (the recipe is in *Matters of Taste*) and my own cheese souf-flés and curries. My food tastes good and is not laden with the preser-vatives of prepackaged frozen or canned products. But I also know that if there is no milk in the house dried milk is a good substitute—and that it is possible to make a more than respectable soufflé out of a can of cream of mushroom soup.

Plan menus for the week. Determine realistically how many meals you will eat at home and how many out. Your food budget will allow more splurge if you plan ahead for pickup meals at home and avoid fast food. A bowl of soup is better, faster, and cheaper than a burger and fries, and healthier. If you view the planning as an ordeal, however, it won't work.

It should be very clear by now that the well-stocked pantry is more than just a collection of convenience foods that can be translated into instant meals, although it's that too. Pantry meals are not necessarily quick meals, but who cares if you can get a pot of bean soup simmering on the stove some snowy Sunday without leaving the house? It is my hope that this book helps you organize your life so you can reduce your shopping trips to a manageable number and eat better than ever in between.

Herbed Vegetable Yogurt Cheese Dip ■ *Eggplant Caviar* ■ *Hummus Dip* ■ *Sesame Cheese Wafers* ■ *Savory Cheese Wafers* ■ *Veal*

WELCOMES
AND
WHETTERS

and Country Ham Pâté ■ *Spicy Sautéed Shrimp* ■ *Spring Rolls* ■ *Artichoke Nibbles* ■ *Skewered Barbecued Shrimp*

IT IS NOT JUST that appetizers welcome and greet, whetting the appetite for more. They are also delaying tactics, a way to keep the guests happy while the host scrounges around for something to serve as the main course.

In a perfect world, one would know exactly who was expected and when so there would be a gracious plenty of time to prepare a suitable welcome. But friends come through town unexpectedly, opportunities to entertain present themselves at the last minute, and a country walk or a stroll on the beach may turn into a more extended visit—one that will eventually require some refreshments.

That's when tasty dips and cheeses and canned delicacies like artichokes and even smoked oysters, long neglected on the shelf, come into play. It's a good idea to have a panic list on the cupboard door, detailing some of the desperation measures held within. Here's a sample: spread hot pepper jelly on cream cheese; open canned smoked oysters and skewer with toothpicks; defrost pâté from the freezer; make yogurt dip and add vegetables; heat canned snails with garlic/herb butter; top goat cheese or cream cheese with slivers of sun-dried tomatoes and oil. When the pressure's on I can't remember these easy things but with a quick jog to the memory I can have a welcoming spread on the table in no time at all.

HERBED VEGETABLE YOGURT CHEESE DIP

This is just one of dozens of ways to use Yogurt Cheese, my latest always-on-hand substitute for all kinds of high-fat foods, like mayonnaise and sour cream. This refreshing dip has just a subtle hint of tanginess. Low in fat and very high in calcium, it makes you feel like you're cheating but you're not. It does not freeze, but it will keep 3 to 5 days in the refrigerator. Who would guess anything so smashing and stunningly attractive and colorful could be so good for you?

3 cups Yogurt Cheese (see sidebar)

1 16-ounce container 1% fat cottage cheese, drained

1 10-ounce package frozen chopped spinach or turnip greens, thawed and squeezed dry

1 roasted red bell pepper (page 106), peeled, seeded, and chopped, or 1 canned pimiento, drained

1 8-ounce can sliced water chestnuts, drained (optional)

3 garlic cloves, peeled and finely chopped

6 green onions, chopped

1 carrot, shredded

1 to 2 tablespoons Pickapeppa hot sauce or 1 teaspoon Tabasco sauce

1 tablespoon drained capers

1 tablespoon chopped basil, preferably fresh

1 tablespoon chopped oregano, preferably fresh

1 tablespoon chopped thyme, preferably fresh

1 tablespoon curry powder

Juice of 2 lemons

Salt

Freshly ground black pepper

In a large bowl, mix together the Yogurt Cheese, cottage cheese, spinach or turnip greens, red bell pepper, water chestnuts, garlic, green onions, carrot, hot sauce, capers, basil, oregano, thyme, curry powder, lemon juice, and salt and pepper to taste. Refrigerate at least 4 hours before serving. Serve with crisp, fresh vegetables, crackers, or toasted pita chips.

Makes 4 cups

EGGPLANT CAVIAR

I first had eggplant caviar in the sixties at the home of a friend whose husband hated eggplant but loved caviar. She said it fooled him every time—he adored this very tasty spread, which is good on pita toast or crisp crackers. I tend to have eggplants around, as I am very fond of ratatouille, and they are good keepers. It is best made a day ahead and keeps 10 days covered and refrigerated, but it does not freeze.

¼ cup olive oil

2 cups chopped celery

2 large onions, chopped

2 large eggplants, peeled and cut into
   1-inch cubes (6 cups)

6 tablespoons red wine vinegar

1 tablespoon sugar

¼ cup tomato paste

2 cups mushrooms, cleaned and sliced

2 tablespoons capers, rinsed and drained

20 large ripe black olives, pitted and
   chopped

¼ cup chopped fresh parsley

Salt

Freshly ground black pepper

Heat the olive oil in a large skillet over medium heat. Add the celery and onions and sauté until the vegetables are crisp-tender, about 10 minutes. Add the eggplants and cook until lightly golden, about 10 minutes. Remove the vegetables with a slotted spoon and set aside.

Add the vinegar, sugar, tomato paste, and mushrooms to the skillet and bring to the boil. Lower the heat and simmer 15 minutes. Return the celery, onion, and eggplant to the skillet. Add the capers, black olives, and parsley. Season to taste with salt and pepper. Stir to combine, cover, and simmer until the eggplant is very tender and the sauce is thick, about 15 minutes. Cool, then refrigerate, covered, for 24 hours before serving.

Makes 5 to 6 cups

HUMMUS DIP

CHICKPEAS
Canned chickpeas are one of the most versatile beans I have on my shelf. Unlike some other varieties, which can be mushy or mealy from the can and are frequently better when reconstituted from dried, chickpeas are almost always firm and fresh tasting right out of the can. Rinse and toss them into a vegetable stew to add protein and substance, sprinkle them over a salad (they blend nicely with olives), or puree them and thin with stock or vegetable juice for an easy, hearty soup.

This chickpea spread has more flavor than the traditional version. Instead of the hard-to-find tahini (sesame seed paste) we have substituted peanut butter (which has the added benefit of lasting a long time on the shelf) for an interesting change of pace. Serve it with raw vegetables or toasted pita wedges. It freezes well for 2 months.

1 15-ounce can chickpeas, drained
¼ cup hot water
2 tablespoons lemon juice
4 garlic cloves, peeled and chopped
¼ cup smooth peanut butter
1 tablespoon dark sesame oil
1 teaspoon ground cumin
½ teaspoon cayenne pepper

Salt
Freshly ground black pepper

GARNISH
4 green onions, chopped
1 tablespoon chopped fresh cilantro
1 tablespoon extra virgin olive oil

Rinse the chickpeas well and put them in the bowl of a food processor. Begin to process, gradually adding the hot water to obtain a light, spreadable consistency. Add the lemon juice, garlic, peanut butter, sesame oil, cumin, and cayenne and season to taste with salt and pepper. Process until well blended and smooth. Mound the spread into a serving bowl or on a platter surrounded by pita chips. Sprinkle with the green onions, cilantro, and olive oil.

Makes 2 cups

SESAME CHEESE WAFERS

No one would guess how easy these are to make when they taste this perfect little nibble. Both the dough and the wafers freeze for up to 3 months. Take a frozen log along to the cabin or lake and bake them there, giving a homemade smell to a strange place.

¾ cup crumbled blue cheese (4 ounces)
1 cup loosely packed shredded cheddar
  cheese (4 ounces)
½ cup (1 stick) butter, softened

½ teaspoon cayenne pepper
1 cup all-purpose flour
3 tablespoons toasted sesame seeds

In a mixer bowl, beat together the blue cheese, cheddar cheese, and butter until smooth. Add the cayenne, flour, and sesame seeds and beat until blended. Shape the dough into long rolls, about 1½ to 2 inches in diameter. Wrap well and refrigerate until firm, at least 1 hour. The rolls may be frozen at this point and sliced and baked later.

Preheat the oven to 350°F.

Unwrap the dough and cut the log into ¼-inch-thick slices. Arrange the slices on an ungreased baking sheet, leaving about 1 inch between the slices. Bake until they show a slight browning around the edges, 12 to 14 minutes. Cool the wafers on the baking sheet for 2 minutes, then transfer them to a rack to cool. Store in an airtight container for 2 or 3 days.

Makes 3 dozen

WHOLE VERSUS GROUND SPICES

The flavor of spices in their whole, or seed form—including cumin, mustard, and fennel seeds—is a bit more subtle and less sharp than when they are ground. Whole lasts longer than ground as well. (Ground really should be replaced every 6 months!) To bring out their fullest flavor and enticing aroma, whole spices are best macerated in a liquid, such as a dressing, which draws their flavor out, or gently heated, either by toasting in a dry skillet or sautéing in oil. To grind spices, use a pepper grinder. Sometimes an electric coffee grinder works, as well.

SAVORY CHEESE WAFERS

CHEESE IN A CAN
Brie and Camembert cheeses can be purchased in cans and are good to keep on hand. They are not as wonderful as top quality, fresh and aged to perfection, but on a cold winter's night they are lovely popped into a hot oven or the microwave to melt and served with French bread, rusks, or crackers by themselves or topping a bowl of onion soup. Straight from the can they can even substitute for cream cheese or goat cheese and can be topped or split and sandwiched with dried apricots or other dried fruits to make a very fetching hors d'oeuvre. They can also be wrapped with bread or pastry dough and baked for quite an elegant surprise.

Crispy and cheesy, these are ideal little munchies or treats for guests. If you've got cream cheese in the freezer, you'll be able to make these at the drop of a hat, using whatever odds and ends of cheese are lurking in your refrigerator. Just allow time for the dough to firm up before baking them. They can be frozen for 2 months.

1 cup (2 sticks) butter, at room temperature
1 8-ounce package cream cheese, at room temperature
2 tablespoons Dijon mustard
1 to 2 teaspoons hot red pepper flakes
1 teaspoon salt
1 teaspoon freshly ground black pepper
2 garlic cloves, peeled and finely chopped
1½ cups grated sharp cheddar cheese (¼ pound)
1½ cups crumbled blue cheese
2 cups whole wheat flour
2 tablespoons cornstarch

Preheat the oven to 350°F.

In a mixing bowl, beat together the butter, cream cheese, and mustard. Stir in the pepper flakes, salt, pepper, and garlic. Add the cheddar and blue cheeses, stirring until well combined.

In a separate bowl, sift together the whole wheat flour and cornstarch. Add to the cheese mixture, stirring just enough to blend them evenly. Turn the dough onto a sheet of plastic wrap about 18 inches long, flour it lightly, and shape it into a log. Roll it tightly in the plastic wrap, making a round tube of dough about 16 inches long. Refrigerate for at least 1 hour.

Unwrap the dough and cut the log into ¼-inch-thick slices. Arrange the slices on an ungreased baking sheet, leaving about 1 inch between the slices. Bake until they show a slight browning around the edges, 15 to 20 minutes. Cool the wafers on the baking sheet for 2 minutes, then transfer them to a rack to cool. Store in an airtight container for 2 or 3 days.

Makes 5 dozen

VEAL AND COUNTRY HAM PÂTÉ

This pâté is the best garden variety pâté. When I see ground veal on sale, I buy it and freeze it for this recipe, but ground turkey or chicken works fine, too. It's not exotic but it is great tasting if you are sure to taste for seasoning before baking. The pistachios add color and texture, but are certainly expendable. The small French gherkins known as cornichons and mustard are the traditional accompaniments. The cooked loaf freezes for 2 months.

2 pounds ground veal, turkey, or chicken or a combination
½ pound country ham, cut into ½-inch cubes
2 pounds ground pork
1 teaspoon freshly grated nutmeg
1 teaspoon ground allspice
1 tablespoon chopped fresh basil
1 tablespoon chopped fresh thyme
1 tablespoon chopped sage
1 teaspoon freshly ground black pepper
1 teaspoon cayenne pepper
1 teaspoon salt

2 large onions, chopped
6 garlic cloves, peeled and chopped
½ cup breadcrumbs
2 eggs, beaten
¼ cup red wine
¼ cup dry sherry
¼ cup cognac, brandy, or Armagnac
1½ cups shelled pistachios (optional)
1 pound thinly sliced bacon

Cornichons
Hot mustard

Preheat the oven to 350°F.

In a large bowl, combine the ground veal, cubed ham, ground pork, nutmeg, allspice, basil, thyme, sage, black pepper, cayenne, salt, onions, garlic, breadcrumbs, eggs, red wine, sherry, and cognac. Stir together thoroughly, using your hands if need be. Mix in the pistachio nuts if using. Form a small amount into a patty and fry it in a skillet over medium heat. When cooked through (it should be completely opaque and white inside) and cooled, taste it and adjust your seasonings accordingly. The pâté needs assertive seasonings since it is served chilled.

Line the bottom and sides of a 5-cup loaf or pâté pan with strips of bacon, overlapping slightly and allowing the ends of the bacon to hang over the edge. Press the filling into the pan and fold the bacon back over the top of the meat. Cover any exposed pâté with extra bacon strips. Put the pan on a baking sheet and place in the oven. Bake until the juices are clear, about 1½ hours. Remove from the oven and let cool. Carefully drain off the fats and juices. Cover with foil, top with a 2-pound weight (this will compress the pâté), and refrigerate for 12 to 24 hours before serving. Slice into ½-inch-thick slices and serve with cornichons and hot mustard.

Makes 15 slices

SPICY SAUTÉED SHRIMP

This quick and easy first course is not only perfect for stand-up parties, it is also good served over pasta as a main dish for 4. (Double the sauce ingredients if serving over pasta.)

¼ cup (½ stick) butter
1 teaspoon curry powder
1 teaspoon ground cumin seeds
1 teaspoon ground coriander seeds
1 teaspoon ground fennel seeds

1 tablespoon lemon juice
Salt
Freshly ground black pepper
*1 pound medium-large shrimp, fresh or
    frozen, peeled*

Melt the butter in a large skillet. Add the curry powder, cumin, coriander, fennel, and lemon juice. Reduce the heat to low and cook gently 10 to 15 minutes to marry and soften the flavors. Add salt and pepper to taste. Add the shrimp to the skillet and toss to coat well with the spices. Raise the heat to medium and cook, turning once, until just done, about 4 minutes total. Skewer with toothpicks and serve.

Serves 4 to 6

FROZEN SHRIMP
Whether you buy it frozen or freeze your own, shrimp is an elegant staple to have for impromptu entertaining. Most of the shrimp available at the fish market has been frozen and defrosted. It may be refrozen if still fresh smelling. I resist buying packages of frozen shrimp because I like seeing the quality if possible.
   To freeze shrimp, put some water in a freezer container, fill the container three-quarters full with the shrimp, and cover with additional water, leaving some room for expansion. Cover tightly and freeze. Defrost in the refrigerator overnight or in the microwave.

SPRING ROLLS

Egg rolls are a double-crunch treat—first the hot, crispy wrapper, and then the natural crunch of the cabbage, carrots, and sprouts. I never buy anything especially to fill the egg rolls; I just use what's in the refrigerator—a little bit of this, a little of that. This is a good use for leftover cooked chicken, but it can be omitted if there is none in the house. Ground or shredded pork is a good substitute. Napa cabbage is best, but regular green cabbage will do fine.

1 tablespoon vegetable oil

1 garlic clove, peeled and chopped

1 tablespoon chopped fresh ginger

¾ cup cooked, shredded chicken or pork

¾ cup finely chopped Napa or regular
   green cabbage

¾ cups canned or fresh mung bean
   sprouts (optional)

¾ cup grated carrots

4 scallions or green onions, chopped

3 tablespoons soy sauce

Salt

Freshly ground black pepper

½ pound won ton wrappers, thawed

Peanut or vegetable oil for frying

Dipping Sauce (page 112)

Heat the oil in a large skillet over medium-high heat. Add the garlic and ginger and sauté briefly. Add the chicken, cabbage, bean sprouts if using, carrots, scallions, soy sauce, and salt and pepper to taste. Stir-fry over high heat, tossing briskly until the vegetables are cooked and all the liquid has evaporated, 3 to 5 minutes. Cool to room temperature to prevent the wrapper from becoming soggy.

Place 1 tablespoon of the filling in the center of each wrapper. Moisten the edges of the wrapper with a little water, fold 2 opposite edges in toward the center just a little, and then roll the wrapper over the filling, beginning and ending with the unfolded edges. Moisten the flap to seal it and let the roll dry so that it won't come apart when fried.

Heat 1 inch of oil in a large Dutch oven to 375°F. Fry the spring rolls about 2 minutes, until golden brown. Turn them over with tongs and fry another 2 minutes. Remove the rolls from the oil with a slotted spoon or tongs and hold

WRAPPERS
Won ton wrappers (a square form of pasta) are found in refrigerator cases at large grocery stores or Asian specialty shops. I buy them fresh and freeze until needed. They defrost in a few minutes when separated. Fried and sliced, they can be sprinkled with curry powder, five-spice powder, or confectioners' sugar and will last, tightly covered, several days at room temperature or will freeze. They are also quite tasty sprinkled with salt, but the salt will, of course, make them soggy after an hour or so. Like egg roll skins, they can enclose any number of finely chopped ingredients, and can be poached or fried, whether shaped like a nun's cap or a beggar's purse.

in a vertical position to allow the oil in the creases to run out. Drain on paper towels. Serve immediately with Dipping Sauce.

Makes 20 to 25 egg rolls

NOTE: I chop everything and even fill the wrappers the night before or early in the day. The actual frying takes no time.

ARTICHOKE NIBBLES

My friends especially love this cheesy artichoke finger food—I do, too! Baked in a pan and cut in squares, it's so nice for cocktail parties. For individual servings, bake the mixture in mini muffin tins and reduce the cooking time to 20 minutes. This freezes well for 2 to 3 months.

2 tablespoons olive oil
1 medium onion, finely chopped
1 to 2 garlic cloves, peeled and finely chopped
2 6-ounce jars marinated artichoke hearts, drained and chopped
4 eggs, lightly beaten

1 teaspoon salt
1/3 cup fine dry breadcrumbs
Freshly ground black pepper
1/4 teaspoon Tabasco sauce
1/2 pound sharp cheddar cheese, grated
2 tablespoons finely chopped fresh parsley
1 tablespoon finely chopped fresh oregano

Preheat the oven to 325°F. Grease a 9-inch square baking pan and set aside.

Heat the olive oil in a frying pan over medium-high heat, add the onion and garlic, and cook until soft, about 5 minutes. In a medium mixing bowl, combine the sautéed onions with the artichoke hearts, eggs, salt, breadcrumbs, pepper, Tabasco, cheese, parsley, and oregano. Mix well and pour into the prepared pan.

Bake 30 to 35 minutes, or until set in the center when lightly touched. Let cool in the pan and cut into 1-inch squares.

Serves 8 to 10

SKEWERED BARBECUED SHRIMP

My friend Karen Lee has written several remarkable cookbooks. I particularly was impressed with this recipe that she served me from *Nouvelle Chinese Cooking*. It's so easy, and when I invite people over for a quick bite before we go out to supper, it's a perfect little "snack" that holds them until we get where we are going. I've used it as an entrée for 8 people, too, served over rice.

2 tablespoons peanut oil	1 cup dark brown sugar
3½ tablespoons chopped ginger	½ cup soy sauce
8 garlic cloves, peeled and chopped	¼ cup rice or wine vinegar
1 cup tomato sauce	2 tablespoons hot sauce
½ cup dry sherry	4 pounds medium shrimp, shelled

Heat a wok or large frying pan over high heat until it smokes. Add the peanut oil, then the ginger, reduce the heat and add the garlic. Stir in the tomato sauce, sherry, sugar, soy sauce, vinegar, and hot sauce. Bring the sauce to the boil, stirring until the sauce has thickened. Remove the sauce from the pan and cool. Add the shrimp. Marinate in the refrigerator, covered, 8 hours if possible. (I use a plastic zip-type bag.)

When ready to serve, remove the shrimp from the marinade, shake off the excess, and thread onto skewers. Prepare a charcoal grill or preheat the broiler. Grill or broil the shrimp on one side until pink. Turn and cook no more than a few minutes, until they are just cooked through. Bring the remaining marinade up to the boil and serve with the shrimp and plenty of hot bread.

Serves 16

Autumn Curried Soup ■ *Lentil Chili Topped with Corn Bread* ■ *Chili Sin Carne* ■ *Dave's Deluxe Gift Corn Chowder* ■ *Leek and Potato Soup with Country Ham* ■ *Corn and Sweet Potato Chowder* ■ *Scalloped Onion and*

MEALS IN A BOWL

Potato Soup ■ *Clean Out the Refrigerator Minestrone* ■ *Hearty Celery Soup* ■ *Puree of Onion Soup* ■ *Minted Pea Soup* ■ *Asparagus Soup* ■ *Curried Cream of Tomato Soup* ■ *Thick and Hearty Tomato Herb Soup*

SOUPS USED TO BE thought of as mainly starters or lunch meals. Now, give me some fresh bread, a bowl of soup, and perhaps a salad, and I'm happy.

Some soups lend themselves to elegance as starters, such as Asparagus Soup or Curried Cream of Tomato Soup. Others, like the Thick and Hearty Tomato Herb Soup and Dave's Deluxe Gift Corn Chowder, are able to accompany a sandwich and salad as a lunch or Sunday night supper in themselves. Many of these ingredients come completely from the shelf or the freezer, but even the most jaded friend wouldn't guess if you had the fire lit and the table set fetchingly.

Chili sin Carne freezes so well I keep it in individual serving-sized plastic bags in the freezer as a treat that I can have for myself on lonely cold nights or for a desperation meal when unexpected guests expand the horizons.

Taste different stocks or broths—from bouillon cubes, granules, and cans—beef, chicken, and vegetable—to determine which you like the most and want to keep on your shelves. I tend to prefer canned stock when I can't have fresh. Many times I dilute it with water. But when I am toting groceries on vacation for the weekend and car space is small, I use the granules or cubes.

Plain stock from a can is easily dressed up. Add noodles, freshly chopped ginger, canned shrimp or crab, potatoes, rice, dried spices or herbs, curry powder, or what have you—leftover vegetables or cooked meats—and you have a meal!

AUTUMN CURRIED SOUP

HARDY SQUASH

All the hard squashes, such as butternut, Hubbard, delicata, and acorn, are extremely sturdy and will last almost as long as onions and potatoes if stored in a cool, well-ventilated spot. In fact they keep so well you may buy them and then forget you have them! That's a shame, though, because they are a good source of vitamins A and C and have many uses. Steam and then puree the squash for a quick but savory side dish, chunk them into soups and stews, or bake slices in the oven to accompany roasted meats.

Here's another great way to use canned, unseasoned pumpkin puree, a vitamin A-rich vegetable that should be in your cabinet year round—not just at the holidays. Acorn squash keeps almost as well as the canned pumpkin. Fall flavors burst from this thick and rich soup, which freezes up to 4 months.

¼ cup (½ stick) butter	¼ to ½ teaspoon ground cinnamon
3 onions, sliced	Salt
4 garlic cloves, peeled and chopped	Freshly ground black pepper
2 tablespoons chopped fresh rosemary	1 16-ounce can solid pack pumpkin
2 acorn squash, peeled, seeded, and cubed	8 cups fresh or canned chicken stock or broth
3 pounds carrots, peeled and sliced	Grated peel (no white attached) of 2 oranges
1½ tablespoons curry powder	½ cup orange juice
2 teaspoons ground cumin	2 cups heavy cream (optional)
1 teaspoon ground coriander	

In a large pot, melt the butter over medium heat. Add the onions, garlic, and rosemary and cook until soft, about 5 minutes. Add the squash, carrots, curry powder, cumin, coriander, and cinnamon. Season to taste with salt and pepper. Cook for 15 minutes, stirring occasionally. Add the pumpkin, chicken stock, orange peel, and juice and cook until the carrots are soft, about 20 minutes longer. Remove from the heat and puree in batches until smooth. Return to the pot, add the cream if desired, and cook until just heated through. Adjust the seasonings and serve hot.

Serves 12

LENTIL CHILI TOPPED WITH CORN BREAD

When this pops out of the oven, no one will guess it's made with lentils from the shelf! It's very tasty. I've made the base ahead, frozen it, defrosted it in the microwave, then turned it into a pie dish, topped it with the cornmeal mixture, and put it in the oven. Use canned or dried lentils.

2 tablespoons vegetable oil

2 medium onions, chopped

2 red and/or green bell peppers, chopped

4 celery stalks, chopped

3 garlic cloves, peeled and chopped

3 to 4 tablespoons chili powder

1 tablespoon ground cumin

1 teaspoon dried oregano

½ teaspoon ground ginger

4 cups fresh or canned chicken stock or broth

2 cups cooked lentils, rinsed

1 1-pound can whole tomatoes, coarsely chopped

Salt

Freshly ground black pepper

CRUST

1 cup self-rising soft wheat flour

1 cup cornmeal

1 egg

1 cup buttermilk

¼ cup vegetable oil

Preheat the oven to 400°F.

In a large Dutch oven, heat the oil. Add the onions, peppers, and celery and cook over medium heat until soft, about 8 to 10 minutes. Add the garlic and cook 2 to 3 minutes more. Stir in the chili powder, cumin, oregano, and ginger. Cook 1 to 2 minutes. Add the chicken stock, lentils, and tomatoes. Bring to the boil, reduce the heat, and simmer for 45 to 50 minutes. Season to taste with salt and pepper. Place in an ovenproof serving dish or pie plate.

In a medium mixing bowl, stir together the flour and cornmeal. Whisk together the egg, buttermilk, and oil and stir into the flour mixture until just blended. Spoon the corn bread mixture on top of the chili and bake 25 to 30 minutes. Let the casserole stand for 10 minutes before cutting into wedges and serving.

Serves 8

CHILI SIN CARNE

This is a simply delicious meatless chili recipe from my friend Marjorie Nunn. The green peppers add some snap and texture but can certainly be omitted if there are none in the crisper; otherwise this one can be made right off the shelves. Eat it hot in a bowl by itself, over rice, or spoon into pita bread. I fix chili on cold, rainy days, relishing it, then freeze leftovers in small containers for those times when I need a quick microwavable meal. At the beach or mountains, it's particularly welcome for lunch or an early supper. It freezes up to 3 months.

3 tablespoons olive oil

2 medium onions, chopped

2 garlic cloves, peeled and finely chopped

3 tablespoons chili powder

$\frac{1}{2}$ teaspoon dried thyme

$\frac{1}{2}$ teaspoon dried oregano

1 tablespoon ground cumin

2 carrots, peeled and finely chopped

2 green bell peppers, seeded and chopped

1 14$\frac{1}{2}$-ounce can tomatoes, drained and chopped

1 15-ounce can kidney beans, undrained

2 15-ounce cans kidney beans, drained and thoroughly rinsed

1 15-ounce can black beans, undrained

1$\frac{1}{2}$ cups fresh or canned beef stock or broth

Salt

Freshly ground black pepper

Cooked white rice

In a large pot, heat the olive oil over medium-high heat. Add the onions and garlic and sauté until soft, 4 to 5 minutes. Stir in the chili powder, thyme, oregano, and cumin, then add the carrots and peppers and cook for 5 minutes, stirring occasionally. Stir in the chopped tomatoes, undrained kidney beans, drained kidney beans, black beans, and stock. Bring to the boil. Reduce the heat and simmer until thick, 30 to 45 minutes. Season to taste with salt and pepper. Serve hot over rice.

Serves 8

DAVE'S DELUXE GIFT CORN CHOWDER

David Sylvain (who does all our computer hand-holding) grew up in Kennebec County, Maine. He sends quarts of this soup as holiday gifts. (It was frozen and sent express overnight from Atlanta to Dave's sister Claudia in California.) This chowder can be made entirely from the bomb shelter basics if you choose to use canned potatoes and use powdered milk for the fresh. It develops a unique character all its own and does not take on the flavor of any one of its ingredients. David says the recipe has been shared with many but followed by few. However, the garlic and lean salt pork, as well as the evaporated milk, are essential to its success. It can be frozen up to 4 months, although it freezes better without the potatoes. Thaw overnight in the refrigerator and reheat gently over low heat, stirring to prevent scorching.

CREAM-STYLE CORN
Cream-style corn is a different vegetable altogether from fresh corn or even frozen. I love both, but cream-style has a special place in my repertoire. It is very welcome on cool summer nights, for instance, as a side dish. Add a few chopped fresh herbs and it's a gourmet delight.

½ pound very lean salt pork (streak-o-lean) or bacon, cut into ½-inch cubes

1 large onion, chopped

2 garlic cloves, peeled and finely chopped

¼ teaspoon curry powder

6 medium-large russet or baking potatoes or 3 16-ounce cans potatoes, drained and cut into 1-inch cubes

1 teaspoon salt

1 teaspoon chopped tarragon

3 16½-ounce cans cream-style corn

2 15-ounce cans evaporated milk

1 quart milk

½ teaspoon lemon pepper

2 tablespoons butter

1 to 2 tablespoons sugar (optional)

In a large skillet, fry the salt pork over medium heat until nearly crisp. Remove it with a slotted spoon and reserve. Drain off all but 2 tablespoons of fat or enough to cover the bottom of the pan. Reduce the heat to low and add the onion, garlic, and curry powder. Sauté until the onion and garlic are soft, about 12 minutes.

Meanwhile, peel the potatoes and cut them into medium-size irregular chunks. Add the potatoes to a 5-quart pot with the salt, tarragon, and enough water to cover the potatoes by 1 inch. Bring to the boil and cook the potatoes for 15 minutes. Drain off all the water, then add the corn, both evaporated and fresh milks, onion mixture, reserved salt pork, lemon pepper, butter, and sugar if desired. Simmer, covered, until thickened, 1 to 1½ hours. Add more milk as needed. Cool and refrigerate, covered, overnight. Serve the next day very warm but not hot.

Makes 15 to 20 cups

LEEK AND POTATO SOUP WITH COUNTRY HAM

This hearty, colorful winter soup derives a great deal of flavor from a blend of toasted seeds. The soup can be pureed for a dressier presentation.

1 teaspoon cumin seeds
1 teaspoon caraway seeds
1 teaspoon fennel seeds
3 tablespoons olive oil
6 leeks, thinly sliced (about 4 cups)
10 to 12 potatoes, peeled and cut into
 ½-inch pieces

1 cup country ham, cut into ½-inch
 pieces
10 cups fresh or canned chicken stock or
 broth
3 cups thinly sliced red cabbage
Salt
Freshly ground black pepper

In a large stockpot, heat the cumin, caraway, and fennel seeds over medium heat until lightly toasted and fragrant; do not burn. Remove from the pan and set aside.

In a large pot, heat the oil over medium-low heat. Add the leeks and cook until soft, about 5 minutes. Add the potatoes, ham, and stock. Bring to the boil, and then add the cabbage and reserved seeds. Reduce the heat and simmer until the potatoes are tender, about 15 minutes. Season to taste with salt and pepper.

Serves 10 to 12

N O T E: *If there is no ham available, sauté 4 to 6 strips of bacon until nearly crisp, drain, chop, and add to the soup.*

CORN AND SWEET POTATO CHOWDER

A couple of days before Thanksgiving, one of my assistants started cleaning out the pantry, fridge, and freezer for the holidays. It was a cold, rainy afternoon and he devised this hearty soup with what he found in cold storage. Add corn bread and poached fruit for a quick and easy meal. It freezes for 2 months.

8 slices bacon

1 onion, chopped

2 celery stalks, chopped

2 garlic cloves, peeled and chopped

1 carrot, chopped

1 tablespoon chopped fresh or dried rosemary

¼ cup chopped fresh parsley

2 tablespoons all-purpose flour

1 tablespoon curry powder

6 to 8 cups fresh or canned chicken stock or broth

1 roasted red bell pepper (page 106), chopped

3 sweet potatoes, peeled and cubed

1 16-ounce package frozen white or yellow corn

Salt

Freshly ground black pepper

1 to 2 teaspoons sugar (optional)

In a Dutch oven, fry the bacon over medium heat until crisp. Remove from the pan, drain on paper towels, crumble, and set aside.

Pour off all but 3 tablespoons of the bacon drippings from the pan and add the onion, celery, garlic, carrot, rosemary, and parsley. Cook over medium heat, stirring occasionally, until the vegetables are golden brown and caramelized, about 20 minutes. Add the flour and curry powder and cook 3 minutes longer. Add the chicken stock, red bell pepper, sweet potatoes, and corn. Season to taste with salt and pepper. Bring to the boil, cover, and simmer until the potatoes are tender, 15 to 20 minutes. Taste and adjust the seasonings, adding the sugar if desired. Garnish with the crumbled bacon.

Serves 8

SIDE MEAT
Nowhere is the smoky flavor of bacon more appreciated than in a soup, where just a bit adds depth and intensity of flavor to other milder ingredients. If you don't have bacon, any of the following can stand in: salt pork, streak-o-lean, prosciutto, country ham.

SCALLOPED ONION AND POTATO SOUP

One day I had an inordinate craving for scalloped potatoes, but I also wanted some hot soup for a head cold that was making me miserable. I combined the two ideas and loved the result—a rich soup worth going to bed and staying there for! Serve with French bread or rolls.

6 tablespoons (¾ stick) butter

3 large onions, thinly sliced (about 6 to 8 cups)

2 potatoes, thinly sliced

4 cups fresh or canned beef stock or broth

2 cups water

3 cups heavy cream

Salt

Freshly ground black pepper

2 to 3 cups grated imported Parmesan and Swiss cheeses, mixed together

Melt the butter in a large casserole or pot. Add the onions and cook over medium heat, stirring, until brown and caramel colored, about 15 minutes. Add the potatoes, stock, and water; cover and bring to the boil. Reduce the heat to low and simmer until the potatoes are tender, about 45 minutes. Add the cream and reheat. Season to taste with salt and pepper. Top with the cheeses.

Serves 8

CLEAN OUT THE REFRIGERATOR MINESTRONE

This savory soup was the happy result of combining every last scrap of anything fresh in the refrigerator with dried beans and bacon. Dried mushrooms could easily substitute for the fresh.

2 cups dried Great Northern beans or
    2 16-ounce cans, drained
¼ pound streak-o-lean or bacon,
    chopped
3 medium onions, chopped
7 cups fresh or canned beef or chicken
    stock or broth
3 carrots, cut in large pieces
2 celery stalks, sliced
3 medium potatoes, peeled and cut into
    1-inch pieces
1 eggplant, chopped into 1-inch pieces
    (optional)
2 garlic cloves, peeled and finely chopped

1 14-ounce can whole tomatoes
¾ pound mushrooms, chopped, or
    ½ cup Mushroom Duxelles (page 101)
1 tablespoon salt, or to taste
1 teaspoon freshly ground black pepper,
    or to taste
½ teaspoon cayenne pepper, or to taste
1 teaspoon chopped or crumbled
    rosemary, preferably fresh
½ cup grated imported Parmesan
    cheese
2 tablespoons chopped fresh parsley or
    basil or 2 teaspoons dried thyme or
    oregano

STOCK TIPS
If the world was perfect, we'd all have neatly labeled quarts of concentrates in jars or bottles, or homemade stock in our freezer at all times. In the real world, however, I sometimes have substitutes, especially if I need just a cup or so for rice or sauce. Canned stock is undoubtedly my preference, and I often dilute it with water. Taste the different options, from bouillon cubes and granules—beef, chicken, and vegetable—to determine which you like the most. I use canned clam broth as a fish stock.

Clean and presoak the beans in water to cover by 1 inch for 4 hours or overnight. Drain and rinse.

Combine the streak-o-lean and onions in a large pot and cook over low heat for 10 minutes, stirring occasionally. Add the drained beans, stock, carrots, celery, potatoes, eggplant, and garlic and bring to the boil. Reduce the heat, cover, and simmer 1½ hours. Add the tomatoes, mushrooms, salt, pepper, cayenne, and herbs and simmer for 30 minutes longer. When ready to serve, stir in ¼ cup of the Parmesan and the parsley. Sprinkle additional cheese over the top of each individual serving.

Serves 20

HEARTY CELERY SOUP

Rainy summer days in the country call for a hearty soup as much as winter days do. I like to serve this in a country-style mug with a smattering of bacon, cheese, and celery leaves as garnish and a big thick slice of bread, and that's lunch!

12 slices bacon (preferably thick-sliced
   country-style peppered bacon)
2 onions, sliced
3 cups chopped celery
2 garlic cloves, peeled and chopped
5 cups fresh or canned chicken stock or
   broth, boiling
3 cups milk

1 teaspoon celery seeds
1 to 2 tablespoons chopped fresh thyme
Salt
Freshly grated black pepper

GARNISH
1 cup grated sharp cheddar cheese
1 cup celery leaves, coarsely chopped

In a large skillet, fry the bacon until crisp. Drain on paper towels, crumble into small pieces, and set aside. Pour off all but about 4 tablespoons of the bacon drippings. Add the onions, celery, and garlic and sauté until the onions begin to turn a golden brown, about 10 minutes. In a large stockpot, bring the chicken stock to the boil and then add the sautéed vegetables. Cover and cook for about 20 minutes, or until tender. Strain the vegetable solids, reserving the broth, and puree in a blender or food processor until smooth. Return the pureed mixture to the broth and add the milk, celery seeds, and thyme. Bring to the boil, reduce the heat to a simmer, and cook 5 minutes longer. Adjust the seasonings with salt and pepper to taste. Serve sprinkled with the reserved bacon, cheese, and celery leaves.

Serves 8

PUREE OF ONION SOUP

This rich, thick soup gets its velvety consistency without the help of cream. For an added treat or special occasion, melt some Stilton or blue cheese on slices of toasted French bread and float a crouton on top of each serving. The garlic may be left whole for a more subtle soup. But if you only have chopped garlic in a jar, it can be used instead.

2 tablespoons olive oil

2 pounds yellow onions (about 6), peeled and sliced

1 pound red onions (about 3), peeled and sliced

3 leeks, cleaned and coarsely chopped

10 shallots, peeled and chopped

6 green onions, chopped, green and white parts

12 garlic cloves, peeled

1 bay leaf

1 cup Madeira or dry sherry

8 cups fresh or canned chicken stock or broth

Salt

Freshly ground black pepper

½ cup chopped chives, for garnish

Heat the oil in a 12-inch skillet over medium-low heat. Add the yellow onions, red onions, leeks, shallots, green onions, garlic cloves, and bay leaf and cook, stirring frequently, until the onions are a deep mahogany brown, about 45 minutes. Remove the bay leaf and discard. Transfer the onions to a large (3-quart) stockpot, add the Madeira, and simmer until most of the liquid has evaporated, about 10 minutes. Add the chicken stock and cook, uncovered, until the broth is reduced to 6 cups, about 20 minutes. Transfer the solids to a food processor or blender and process until smooth. Return to the pot and heat to a simmer. Season to taste with salt and pepper. Garnish each serving with the chopped chives.

Serves 4 to 6

MINTED PEA SOUP

INSTANT SOUP

Plain broth or stock from a can is easily dressed up. Add noodles, freshly chopped ginger, canned shrimp or crab, potatoes, rice, dried spices or herbs, curry powder, or what have you—leftover vegetables or cooked meats—and you have a meal!

Here's another elegant soup from the freezer that tastes bright and fresh, and is also very pretty.

¼ cup (½ stick) butter
2 medium onions, finely chopped
2 large garlic cloves, peeled and finely chopped
6 cups fresh or canned chicken stock or broth
1 2½-pound package frozen green peas, thawed

3 to 4 tablespoons finely chopped fresh mint
1 cup heavy cream
Salt
Freshly ground black pepper
Sugar

Melt the butter in a large pot over medium heat. Add the onions and cook until beginning to soften, about 5 minutes. Add the garlic and cook another 3 to 5 minutes; do not brown. Add the stock and peas, bring to the boil, reduce the heat, and simmer 10 to 15 minutes, or until the peas are very soft.

Strain the soup, reserving the broth, and puree the peas and onions in a blender or food processor until smooth. Return the broth and puree to the pan and add the mint and cream. Season to taste with salt, pepper, and sugar. Heat through and serve.

Serves 8 to 10

ASPARAGUS SOUP

Although asparagus has become synonymous with the fleeting pleasures of spring, the vegetable itself is in fact quite sturdy and will keep at least a week in the refrigerator if stored upright with the stems in an inch or so of water. When asparagus is in season, I cook it in great batches. I keep the excess in the refrigerator up to 3 days or freeze them. I use some of the cooked "leftovers" as well as the woody stems for this soup. If you use raw asparagus in this recipe, cook another 10 to 15 minutes to ensure the asparagus is tender enough to puree. The soup will keep up to 3 days in the refrigerator and can be frozen—less the cream—for 2 months.

STORING STOCKS
Undoubtedly you'll have a can or two of chicken and beef broth on your pantry list, but do consider making and freezing your own stock. Freeze stock in 1-quart containers or resealable plastic bags to make measuring easier, always date the container, and use within 3 months. If freezer space is short, boil down the liquid to ice cube size and reconstitute with water when needed.

¼ cup (½ stick) butter

6 green onions, cut into ¼-inch slices

2 pounds asparagus, cooked, tips reserved for garnish

4 cups fresh or canned chicken stock or broth

Salt

Freshly ground black pepper

1½ teaspoons dried tarragon

1 cup heavy cream, half-and-half, or plain yogurt

Melt the butter until sizzling in a medium pot or Dutch oven over medium heat. Add the onions and cook until soft but not brown, 4 to 5 minutes. Add the cooked asparagus, stock, salt, pepper, and tarragon and bring to the boil. Reduce the heat and simmer for 20 minutes. Transfer the vegetables and stock to a blender or food processor and puree until smooth, working in batches if necessary. When ready to eat, bring back to the boil, then reduce the heat to a simmer. Add the cream, making sure it is well incorporated. Taste for seasonings and serve hot, garnished with asparagus tips.

Serves 6 to 8

CURRIED CREAM OF TOMATO SOUP

How does anyone live without canned tomatoes? Surely they are one of the most important ingredients in the house. Combine them with onions and you can always make a meal. In this case, I've created a very tasty soup that's good hot or cold and is ready in no time at all.

6 tablespoons (¾ stick) butter

2 large onions, thinly sliced

1 tablespoon curry powder

2 28-ounce cans plum tomatoes with
  juice

1 cup fresh or canned beef stock

1 cup heavy cream

Sugar

Salt

Freshly ground black pepper

In a large heavy pan, heat the butter over medium heat. Add the sliced onions and curry powder and cook until very soft but not browned, about 8 minutes. Add the tomatoes with their juice and bring to the boil. Reduce the heat and simmer about ½ hour. Working in batches, puree in a blender or food processor until very smooth.

Return the pureed mixture to the pan and add the beef stock and the cream. Heat just until the mixture is heated through. Season to taste with sugar, salt, and pepper and serve hot.

Serves 8

THICK AND HEARTY TOMATO HERB SOUP

With some good bread this is enough for a substantial lunch or Sunday night supper. It makes the house smell so good you'll wish you had doubled it for later in the week.

2 tablespoons butter

1 cup chopped celery (optional)

1 large onion, chopped

1 28-ounce can plum tomatoes, coarsely chopped

2 tablespoons chopped fresh or dried basil

1 tablespoon fresh or dried oregano

1 tablespoon fresh or dried thyme

2 tablespoons chopped fresh parsley

2 bay leaves

4 cups fresh or canned beef stock or broth

Sugar

Salt

Freshly ground black pepper

GARNISH

Approximately 1 cup shaved imported Parmesan cheese (optional)

SHAVED PARMESAN CHEESE
When a more distinctive Parmesan flavor is desired, use a vegetable peeler to shave thin strips off a large chunk of cheese. If you prefer to grate your Parmesan and freeze it rather than keep a wedge in the refrigerator, shave off some shards to store in the freezer before you grate the rest.

In a Dutch oven or large heavy saucepan, melt the butter over medium heat; add the celery and onion and cook until the celery is tender, 7 to 10 minutes. Add the tomatoes, basil, oregano, thyme, parsley, bay leaves, and stock and bring to the boil. Simmer about 30 minutes. Remove from the heat and remove the bay leaves. Puree the soup in batches in a blender or food processor, leaving the soup slightly chunky. Season to taste with sugar, salt, and pepper. Serve hot. Garnish with shaved Parmesan if desired.

Serves 6

Hot Curried Beef with Dried Fruit ■ Beef with Hot Indian Spice and
Spinach ■ Chili Salsa Beef ■ Tart and Tangy Beef on a Bun ■ Steak and

THE MEAT LOCKER

3

Pommes Frites ■ Caribbean Beef Salad ■ Southwestern Ground Beef-Squash
Shells ■ Oven-Barbecued Pork Tenderloin ■ Spicy Pork with Peas ■
Pork Roast with Dried Fruits ■ Sauté of Pork with Apples and Peppers

WITH NEIGHBORHOOD butcher shops dwindling in numbers, more and more of us do most of our meat and poultry shopping at the supermarket, buying in quantity (perhaps a family pack of chops or bulk packages of ground meat) then repackaging it into smaller portions and freezing most of it for future use. Today, a well-stocked freezer is nearly as good, and certainly handier than a neighborhood butcher. With the advent of the microwave, if you've got a pork roast or pound of sausage in the freezer, you'll never be caught without the makings of a festive family meal.

Keeping meat in the freezer is certainly not an innovation. When I lived in Social Circle, each year we would buy part of an animal that had been raised by a young person for Future Farmers of America or 4H. After it was dressed, the meat was placed in the Social Circle meat locker, where, for a negligible fee, I could store it and periodically remove a portion of meat to my home freezer as I had room. Although I was always well supplied with meat, I never seemed to have the particular cut I wanted; out of necessity I learned how flexible different cuts can be. Rounds, chucks, sirloin, and the sirloin tip can all make wonderful roasts, cooked long and slow; alternately, if you cut them thin enough, round and sirloin roasts can produce a pretty good rare steak. Chops can be interchangeable, too, though pork may require longer cooking than lamb chops, which are eaten pink, not well done.

When selecting meat from the freezer, do not be concerned about gray-looking meat; whenever it is exposed to air it will change color.

HOT CURRIED BEEF WITH DRIED FRUIT

CHIVES

Although dried chives work perfectly well, I've developed an affection for the frozen variety. They stay bright green and give an easy touch of color. Buy large bunches at your farmers' market in the summer when they are cheap and freeze them in a resealable plastic bag with all the air pressed out.

This dish is wonderful in the fall when a chill hits the air. It is a lovely dark golden color full of tantalizing flavors and aromas that belie the scant effort involved in its preparation. This recipe is almost better made a couple of days ahead of time. The finished dish can be refrigerated up to 3 days or frozen for 3 months.

3 tablespoons vegetable oil

3 pounds chuck, sirloin tip, or round roast, cut into 2-inch cubes, gristle removed

3 large onions, cut into 1-inch pieces

4 garlic cloves, peeled and chopped

1 tablespoon hot curry powder or Hot Indian Spice (page 114)

1 tablespoon paprika

2 cups mixed dried fruit

½ cup slivered almonds

3 cups fresh or canned beef stock or broth

¼ cup red wine vinegar

Salt

Freshly ground black pepper

4 cups cooked rice

GARNISH

½ cup sour cream (optional) or plain yogurt, drained

3 scallions or green onions, chopped, or 6 tablespoons chopped chives

Over medium-high heat, heat enough of the oil to cover the bottom of a heavy saucepan. Add some of the meat to the pan without crowding and brown it on all sides, turning as necessary, about 5 minutes. Remove it to a plate and set aside. Repeat with the remaining meat, adding additional oil as needed. When all the meat is browned, add the onions, garlic, curry powder, and paprika to the pan and cook until softened, about 5 minutes. Add the dried fruit and almonds, stirring until well mixed. Return the meat to the pan and add the beef stock and red wine vinegar. Season to taste with salt and pepper. Bring to the boil, lower the heat, cover, and simmer for about 1½ hours. Serve on a large platter with the cooked rice. Spoon the pan juices over the meat or pass separately. Garnish with the sour cream if using or yogurt and scallions or chives.

Serves 4 to 6

BEEF WITH HOT INDIAN SPICE AND SPINACH

The mundane becomes memorable with this spicy but not-too-hot adaptation of a recipe from Julie Sahni's book, *Classic Indian Cooking*. If you don't have one of the spices called for, just leave it out. If you only have boneless chicken or turkey on hand, that will work as well as beef.

BROWNING MEAT
Browning larger pieces of meat is quicker and easier than cubes. If you need to, cut the cooked pieces down to a better size for serving, removing any gristle not caught earlier.

2 10-ounce packages frozen spinach, defrosted and drained, or 3 cups cooked fresh spinach, drained

6 tablespoons vegetable oil

3 pounds lean boneless beef, chuck, sirloin tip, or round roast cut into 1½-inch cubes

3½ cups thinly sliced onions

1½ tablespoons finely chopped garlic

3 tablespoons finely chopped fresh ginger

1 tablespoon ground cumin

2 tablespoons ground coriander

1 teaspoon turmeric

1 medium-sized ripe tomato, fresh, frozen, or canned, finely chopped

3 green chiles, fresh or canned, seeded and chopped, or 1 teaspoon red pepper flakes or ground cayenne pepper

3 tablespoons plain yogurt or sour cream

½ teaspoon ground cinnamon

½ teaspoon ground cardamom

½ teaspoon ground cloves

1 tablespoon kosher salt

4 teaspoons Hot Indian Spice (page 114)

Preheat the oven to 325°F.

Finely puree the spinach, using a food processor or electric blender, or finely chop it with a knife on a chopping board. Set aside.

Heat 2 tablespoons of the oil in a large frying pan over high heat until very hot. Dry the meat on paper towels and add enough to cover the bottom of the pan without touching. Brown the meat on one side, then turn and brown on the other, until totally browned. Remove and set aside. Add more beef and repeat until all is browned.

Add the remaining 4 tablespoons oil to the frying pan and add the onions. Lower the heat and cook until they turn a lovely mahogany brown, about 25 minutes, stirring as needed. Add the garlic, ginger, cumin, coriander, and turmeric and cook over low heat for 2 minutes. Add the tomato, reserving the juice if canned, and the chiles and continue cooking until the tomato is cooked and the entire mixture is reduced to a thick pulpy mass, about 5 minutes. Remove from the heat and quickly stir in the yogurt or sour cream. When cool enough to handle, puree in an electric blender or food processor.

Combine the puree and meat in a large skillet. Add the cinnamon, cardamom, and cloves. Stir in 1 cup hot water or the reserved tomato juice along with the salt, distributing the meat into the sauce, and bring to the boil. Add the spinach and Hot Indian Spice and cook 5 more minutes.

Serves 8

CHILI SALSA BEEF

Make your own salsa or use prepared salsa from a jar—either way you'll be pleased with this very snappy meal.

1½ pounds boneless beef chuck shoulder roast
1 tablespoon olive oil
1 cup medium or hot chunky salsa
2 tablespoons packed brown sugar
1 tablespoon soy sauce
1 garlic clove, peeled and chopped
⅓ cup coarsely chopped fresh cilantro (optional) plus springs for garnish
2 tablespoons lime or lemon juice or red wine vinegar
2 cups cooked rice
1 lime, cut crosswise into quarters (optional)

Trim any fat from the beef roast and cut into 1½-inch cubes. In a Dutch oven, heat the oil over medium heat until quite hot. Add the beef and brown on all sides, stirring occasionally. Pour off the drippings if necessary.

Add the salsa, sugar, soy sauce, and garlic to the beef and mix well. Bring to the boil, then reduce the heat to low, cover tightly, and simmer for 1 hour. Uncover and cook 30 minutes longer, or until the beef is tender.

Remove from the heat and stir in the chopped cilantro if using and lime juice. Spoon the beef mixture over the rice and garnish with cilantro sprigs and lime quarters if desired.

Serves 4

TART AND TANGY BEEF ON A BUN

This sloppy Joe-type recipe is popular on the weekends for lunch as well as a quick supper when we feel we "don't have time to eat."

1 pound ground chuck
1 medium onion, chopped
½ cup ketchup
¼ cup packed light or dark brown sugar
¼ cup apple cider vinegar

3 tablespoons Worcestershire sauce
3 tablespoons yellow or Dijon mustard
2 teaspoons honey (optional)
6 hamburger buns

Combine the ground beef and onion in a large skillet and cook over medium heat, breaking up the chunks with a wooden spoon until the meat is browned, about 10 minutes. Drain off the excess fat.

In a small mixing bowl, stir together the ketchup, brown sugar, vinegar, Worcestershire sauce, mustard, and honey if using until well combined. Stir the sauce mixture into the meat and onions and bring to a simmer. Serve on hamburger buns.

Serves 6

STEAK AND POMMES FRITES

My French son-in-law fixes this as a quick supper, so I've learned to keep a few steaks in the freezer. Sirloin is a good cut for the job, but almost any beef cut will work. It's not "politically correct," but it sure is good!

3 tablespoons olive oil
3 potatoes, cut into 1-inch cubes
2 to 3 tablespoons oregano and/or
  thyme, preferably fresh

Salt
Freshly ground black pepper
1 2- to 3-inch-thick top sirloin steak
  (1½ pounds)

Heat enough of the oil to cover the bottom of a large frying pan. Add the potatoes, cook until brown, and turn. Continue to turn until brown all over. Season with oregano and/or thyme, salt, and pepper. Remove with a slotted spoon and drain on paper towels. Keep warm.

Add the steak to the hot fat and cook quickly, about 5 minutes on each side, until brown but rare inside. Let rest on a cutting board for 4 or 5 minutes, then slice rather thickly across the grain and serve with the fried potatoes.

Serves 2 to 3

CARIBBEAN BEEF SALAD

Mangos may not be a pantry staple, but since they are generally sold rock-hard, I have at least a week (longer if, when ripened, I keep it in the fridge) to find a use for it. It's wonderful in salsas for fish or grilled meats, delicious in sorbets, and adds Caribbean zest to this easy salad.

CHUTNEY DRESSING
1 cup plain lowfat yogurt
1/4 cup sour cream
1/3 cup chopped Major Grey's Mango
   Chutney
2 tablespoons apple cider vinegar
1 tablespoon lemon juice
1/8 teaspoon ground allspice

1/8 teaspoon freshly ground black pepper

1 pound deli roast beef, sliced 1/4 inch
   thick
4 cups torn romaine lettuce leaves
1 large mango, peeled and cut into
   3/4-inch cubes
1 red bell pepper, cut into 3/4-inch cubes

To make the dressing, combine the yogurt, sour cream, chutney, vinegar, lemon juice, allspice, and pepper in a medium bowl.

Trim any the fat from the roast beef. Stack the beef slices and cut lengthwise in half and then crosswise into 1/2-inch-wide strips.

To serve, put the lettuce on a serving platter and arrange the beef, mango, and bell pepper on top of the lettuce. Drizzle 1/2 cup dressing over the salad and pass the remaining dressing separately.

Serves 4 to 6

SOUTHWESTERN GROUND BEEF-SQUASH SHELLS

Everyone in my family loves squash. This recipe combines traditional casserole ingredients but is served in individual squash shells. It can be used as a side dish or a main course and it is just perfect for a late Sunday night supper. There are several ways I make this dish work for me. One is to cook the filling, stuff the squash halves, and then refrigerate them until I'm half an hour from eating. Other times I pop them immediately in the oven, using the baking time to make a salad, heat up some soup, and set the table. The stuffed shells will keep 1 to 2 days in the refrigerator. They reheat well in the oven at 325°F. or in the microwave on High.

6 yellow squash or zucchini
2 tablespoons olive oil
1 onion, chopped
3 garlic cloves, peeled and chopped
1 red or green bell pepper, chopped
  (optional)
1 pound ground beef

2 teaspoons ground cumin
1 teaspoon chili powder
½ teaspoon red pepper flakes
½ cup sour cream
½ cup breadcrumbs
¾ cup sharp cheddar cheese
½ cup beef stock

Preheat the oven to 375°F. Grease a 9 × 13-inch baking pan.

Halve the squash and scrape out the seeds. Then scrape or cut out most of the pulp, leaving the sides in tact. In a large skillet, heat the olive oil over medium heat. Add the squash pulp, onion, garlic, and bell pepper if using and cook until soft, about 10 minutes. Remove from the pan and set aside. Add the beef to the same skillet and cook until the pink disappears, about 5 minutes, breaking it up with a wooden spoon. Drain off any additional fat. Add the cumin, chili powder, red pepper flakes, sour cream, breadcrumbs, and cheese to the beef and mix thoroughly. Stir in the sautéed vegetables and combine.

Stuff the hollowed-out squash shells with the mixture.

Place in the prepared pan, pour in the beef stock, and cover the pan. Bake until the squash is soft and the filling is bubbly, about 25 minutes.

Serves 6 to 8

OVEN-BARBECUED PORK TENDERLOIN

This marinade and reduced sauce makes a very palatable entrée that combines several different taste sensations: sweet, tart, and spicy hot. The addition of the citrus juices adds a fresh, clean taste that contrasts nicely with the savory tomato and Worcestershire flavors. The pork makes a delicious cold sandwich the next day.

1 onion, finely chopped
2 garlic cloves, peeled and finely chopped
3 tablespoons tomato paste
3 tablespoons honey
3 tablespoons Worcestershire sauce

3 tablespoons red wine vinegar
½ cup orange juice
3 tablespoons lemon juice
¼ teaspoon cayenne pepper
2 1-pound pork tenderloins

Preheat the oven to 350°F.

In a food processor or blender, combine the onion, garlic, tomato paste, honey, Worcestershire sauce, vinegar, orange juice, lemon juice, and cayenne. Process until you have a thick puree. Pour over the pork tenderloins and marinate if possible at least 6 hours. Remove from the marinade and bake until the pork registers 150°F., about 50 minutes.

Meanwhile, pour the reserved marinade into a shallow pan and bring to the boil. Reduce the heat and simmer until the mixture is thick, about 10 minutes. Pass separately with the pork tenderloins, warm or at room temperature.

Serves 4 to 6

SPICY PORK WITH PEAS

If your pantry is well stocked with Asian ingredients, then you're likely to have everything you need for this colorful stir-fry, so don't be daunted by the lengthy ingredient list. The secret to this and all stir-fries is to have all your ingredients measured and prepped *before* you begin cooking and to cook on high heat. The cooking time is so short that it is critical that ingredients be added quickly, one right after the other, so as not to overcook.

2 tablespoons dry sherry
1 teaspoon red pepper flakes
1 teaspoon Szechuan peppercorns ground (optional)
1 tablespoon cornstarch
¼ cup fresh or canned chicken stock or broth
2 teaspoons sesame oil
¼ cup soy sauce
2 tablespoons oyster sauce
2 teaspoons sugar
3 tablespoons vegetable oil
2½ pounds pork, sliced and cut into thin strips

1 onion, halved and sliced
4 garlic cloves, peeled and chopped
4 quarter-size slices fresh ginger, julienned
2 carrots, julienned
5 green onions, sliced on the diagonal
1½ cups frozen green peas, thawed, or fresh uncooked
2 cups cooked rice
2 tablespoons chopped fresh parsley (optional)
2 canned plum tomatoes or 1 fresh medium tomato, chopped (optional)

In a small bowl, mix together the sherry, red pepper flakes, Szechuan pepper if using, cornstarch, chicken stock, sesame oil, soy sauce, oyster sauce, and sugar. Set aside.

In a large skillet or wok, heat 2 tablespoons of the vegetable oil over high heat until quite hot. Add the pork and cook quickly, tossing until brown all over, about 3 to 4 minutes. Remove to a platter. Add the remaining 1 tablespoon of oil, then the onion, garlic, ginger, carrots, and green onions and quickly sauté until crisp-tender, another 2 to 3 minutes. Add the seasoning mixture to the vegetables and stir until the sauce begins to boil and thicken.

Add the pork and peas to the pan and heat thoroughly, about 1 minute. Serve over steaming rice. Sprinkle with the parsley and chopped tomatoes, if desired.

Serves 4

PORK ROAST WITH DRIED FRUITS

Fruit and pork are a perfect match for ease as well as flavor. This roast is not only fine for company, but the leftovers make great sandwiches. The meat and sauce may be refrigerated up to 3 days and reheated or will freeze up to 4 months. Pork loin may be purchased two ways—either one side of the loin or two sides. This recipe is written for one side. If you have two sides, tie and add 1 hour to the roasting time.

PRESERVED GINGER

Candied ginger can be found in jars in the spice section of the supermarket or in Asian grocery stores in boxes, where it is substantially less expensive. Either way, it keeps virtually forever, and a little goes a long way to add spicy snap to dishes. It's a most worthwhile addition to your baking pantry and it gives many meat dishes flavor and bite, too.

1 3-pound boneless pork loin roast

3 cups fresh or canned chicken broth or stock

¼ cup dried currants, raisins, cherries, or cranberries

2 tablespoons chopped candied ginger

½ cup dried apple, persimmon, or pear slices

1 cup heavy whipping cream or ½ cup (1 stick) butter

Preheat the oven to 375°F.

Place the meat in a large metal roasting pan and roast ½ hour. Mix together the stock, currants, ginger, and fruit and pour around the pork. Continue cooking to an internal temperature of 160°F., about 1½ hours total. Remove the roast to the cutting board, tent with foil, and set aside.

Place the pan over a burner, bring the juices to the boil, and reduce by half, about 10 minutes. Add the cream and boil until thickened, about 7 minutes. If using butter, add room temperature pieces to the warm sauce and do not reboil. Slice the roast and serve the sauce over the pork or pass it separately.

Serves 4 to 6

SAUTÉ OF PORK WITH APPLES AND PEPPERS

This stir-fry is a very simple but substantial entrée. Serve it over rice or couscous and you have a complete meal. The soy sauce adds a certain depth to the flavor of the dish but it doesn't dominate.

2 tablespoons olive oil

2 medium onions, sliced

1 Granny Smith apple, peeled, cored, and cut into 8 wedges (16 if apple is particularly large)

2 red or green bell peppers, sliced ½-inch lengthwise

1 ¾- to 1-pound pork tenderloin, sliced crosswise into ½-inch slices

1 tablespoon soy sauce

¼ cup balsamic or red wine vinegar

½ cup fresh or canned chicken stock or broth

Salt

Freshly ground black pepper

2 to 3 tablespoons finely chopped fresh thyme

2 tablespoons finely chopped fresh parsley

In a large skillet or sauté pan, heat 1 tablespoon of the oil and add the onions, apple, and peppers. Cook over high heat, stirring constantly, until just softened, about 3 to 5 minutes. Remove to a plate and set aside.

Return the pan to the heat. Add the remaining oil and the pork. Brown the meat on one side, then turn it to brown on the other side, 5 minutes total. Move the pork to the bowl with the vegetables. Add the soy sauce, vinegar, and chicken stock to the pan and bring to the boil. Cook until reduced and almost syrupy, about 4 minutes. Add the pork and vegetables and toss well to coat. Season to taste with salt, pepper, thyme, and parsley. Serve at once.

Serves 4 to 6

Crepes with Seafood ■ Mushroom and Oyster Stuffed Crepes ■ Seafood Provençal ■ Fish Pinwheels with Thyme and Parsley ■ Steamed Tilapia and Red Cabbage ■ Smoked Trout Potato Salad with Lemon Vinaigrette ■ Roast Chicken and Zucchini with Moroccan Marinade ■ Chicken Breasts with Dried Apricots and Cranberries ■ Middle

FISH AND POULTRY

Eastern Ratatouille with Grilled Chicken Breast ■ Cornish Hens with Ginger and Marmalade ■ Tangy Chicken Breasts Baked with Black Bean Salsa ■ Chicken Cacciatore ■ Chinese-Style Chicken ■ Maryland Fried Chicken ■ Jozette's Burgundian Godfather's Chicken ■ Turkey Vegetable Loaf ■ Turkey Sausage with Italian Plum Tomatoes and Anchovies

FISH HAS ASSUMED a place of value in the home freezer. Once fish was thought superior when "fresh" (which could mean up to ten days on ice before it arrived at your local fishmonger's!), but I often find fish that has been flash frozen immediately can compare quite favorably with anything but the very freshest fish (usually some I've caught myself or has been donated by a fisherman friend). Some of the varieties I buy frozen are tilapia, orange roughy, and flounder. I look for fish that will be moist when cooked, with no dryness or taste of the freezer. The quality of commercial products varies considerably and is unfortunately a case of trial and error.

Shellfish can also reside quite happily in the freezer, to be tossed into elegant sautés, pasta dishes, and other entrées. Shrimp, crab, and oysters all freeze easily and well. I freeze shrimp in water, but pint containers of shucked clams and oysters are frequently put straight into the freezer, particularly if they come vacuum packed. Crabmeat can also be frozen and defrosted and usually has much better flavor and texture than the canned pasteurized kind.

To freeze fish, either whole or in fillets, dip it in ice water, lay it flat on plastic wrap on a baking sheet, and place in the freezer. When a film of ice has formed, rewrap, refreeze, and pull out as needed. The film of ice seems to keep the fish moist. To freeze shrimp, I have replaced the traditional milk carton with a sawed-off milk or water container. I fill it partially full of water (preferably ocean water), then add the shrimp and continue to fill with water. It should go without saying that shrimp in the shell is preferable to peeled shrimp.

The fat under the shell guarantees a moister end result.

Poultry is a favorite with me, and I always buy chicken when I do a major grocery shop, usually a whole one for roasting and one for stock, soup, or cooked meat. As soon as I get home with my groceries, I put a chicken on to poach, cleaning out my freezer and refrigerator as I go, adding odds and ends to the pot. I bone the chicken breasts, adding their bones to the broth, then freeze the boned breasts flat on a baking sheet before putting them in a freezer container so they can be pulled out individually and used. When the poaching chicken is cooked I remove the flesh, which I freeze or store in the refrigerator. By this point all that is left is the poaching liquid, which has become a savory soup stock that can be strained and frozen.

Cornish hens are especially welcome in the freezer. Like chicken and turkey, the package of the neck, heart, and liver should be removed before rewrapping and freezing. Other small fowl such as quail can easily be defrosted for quick popular main courses or appetite whetters.

My mail reflects an ongoing concern about when poultry and fish may be frozen if it was purchased icy or defrosted by the grocery store. As long as fish and poultry have been maintained at 40°F. or iced down properly and have no odor or other indicators of deterioration, they can safely be refrozen. There will be some loss of quality, but it is not always discernible and is worth the risk.

CREPES WITH SEAFOOD

Crepes are wonderfully elegant looking—and easily accommodate left-overs or even canned or frozen seafood. Add a bit of green and a bit of dairy, a white sauce or even a canned cream soup, and you wind up with something very impressive. Canned seafood can be used in this recipe; just drain it well first.

1 tablespoon butter
2 tablespoons finely chopped onion
1 cup cooked crabmeat, peeled shrimp, or salmon
1/4 cup heavy cream, cream cheese, sour cream, plain yogurt, white sauce, or canned cream soup
1/3 cup grated imported Parmesan cheese

1/3 cup chopped fresh parsley, spinach, or broccoli
1/3 cup breadcrumbs
Salt
Freshly ground black pepper
6 crepes (page 150), warm or at room temperature

Melt the butter in a large frying pan. Add the onion and sauté until tender, about 5 minutes. Stir in the crabmeat (or other seafood), cream, cheese, parsley, and breadcrumbs. Season to taste with salt and pepper. Stir the mixture over medium heat until heated through, 3 to 5 minutes. If using sour cream or yogurt, do not boil.

Put about 1/4 cup filling on each crepe and roll up loosely. Serve immediately or cover and heat in a 350°F. oven until hot throughout.

Serves 2 to 3

CREAM SUBSTITUTES
Ultrapasteurized heavy cream can keep up to a month in the refrigerator, depending on how old it was when you bought it. However, in the absence of cream, there are perfectly acceptable substitutes, including unflavored (plain) yogurt and canned evaporated skim milk. Both are lower in fat than heavy cream in addition to their long shelf lives. Evaporated skim milk can be used in soups, sauces, and coffee. Yogurt gives soups a distinct tang, but must be added with care to prevent it from curdling. Bring the yogurt to room temperature before adding it to hot mixtures. Stir a small amount of the hot mixture into the yogurt first, then combine that mixture with the remaining hot mixture. Do not boil.

MUSHROOM AND OYSTER STUFFED CREPES

Canned oysters do fine with some duxelles from the freezer for this elegant main course or starter.

1 tablespoon butter

1 tablespoon all-purpose flour

1 8-ounce can oysters, drained, liquor
   reserved

¼ cup cream

½ cup Mushroom Duxelles (page 101)

Salt

Freshly ground white pepper

6 crepes (page 150)

2 tablespoons chopped fresh thyme,
   marjoram, or parsley (optional)

Melt the butter in a frying pan. Add the flour and stir to make a smooth roux. Add the oyster liquor and stir until smooth. Add the cream and duxelles, bring to the boil, reduce the heat, and simmer until the mixture thickens slightly, about 2 minutes. Stir in the oysters and just heat through, about 2 minutes longer. Season to taste with salt and pepper.

Fill each crepe with about ¼ cup filling and roll up loosely. Serve immediately or heat in a 350° F. oven until heated through, about 5 minutes. Any leftover sauce can be spooned over the warm crepes. Dust with fresh chopped herbs if you have them.

Serves 2 to 3

SEAFOOD PROVENÇAL

Throw together a quick tomato sauce, add some defrosted scallops or shrimp, and you have a dish fit for a queen! Serve by itself, over pasta, rice, or couscous, or in crepes. It doesn't freeze well, but will reheat if made ahead up to 24 hours.

1 tablespoon olive oil

8 shallots or 1 onion, finely chopped

4 green onions, chopped

2 to 4 garlic cloves, peeled and finely chopped

1 28-ounce can plum tomatoes, slightly broken up

½ cup pitted and chopped black olives, preferably Kalamata (Greek), French, or Italian

1 tablespoon finely chopped basil, preferably fresh

1 tablespoon chopped thyme, preferably fresh

1 pound sea scallops or shrimp, rinsed and patted dry

2 tablespoons lemon juice

Salt

Freshly ground black pepper

2 tablespoons grated orange or lemon peel (no white attached) (optional)

In a large skillet, heat the olive oil and cook the shallots and green onions until beginning to soften, 3 to 4 minutes. Add the garlic and cook an additional 1 to 2 minutes. Add the tomatoes and olives and simmer over medium-low heat until beginning to thicken, about 4 minutes. Add the basil and thyme and cook for 1 minute. Add the scallops or shrimp and cook until opaque and firm to the touch, about 3 to 4 minutes. Season to taste with lemon juice, salt, and pepper. Just before serving, sprinkle with the orange or lemon peel if using.

Serves 4

FISH PINWHEELS WITH THYME AND PARSLEY

This is a pretty presentation that requires hardly any effort on your part. It is best served fresh and hot from the oven with couscous and steamed vegetables. The pinwheels can be made several hours ahead of mealtime. If you use thicker fillets, such as tilapia, put them between two pieces of plastic wrap and pound them to about ¼ inch thick. Store, covered, in the refrigerator and pop in the oven just before serving. If green onions are not available, tie with string and remove before serving. This dish cannot be frozen.

¼ cup finely chopped thyme, preferably
  fresh
¼ cup finely chopped parsley, preferably
  fresh
Salt
Freshly ground black pepper

6 flounder, sole, or other fish fillets
6 green onions, green part only
¼ cup vermouth
2 tablespoons chicken stock or other
  liquid

Preheat the oven to 375°F.

In a small bowl, combine the thyme, parsley, and salt and pepper. Sprinkle each fillet with the herb mixture and roll up so that the herbs are on the inside like a pinwheel. Use the long stems from a green onion to tie each pinwheel together, forming a bundle. Place them in a 6 × 8-inch glass baking dish. Pour the vermouth and chicken stock over the bundles. Bake until the fish flakes easily when pierced with a fork, about 15 minutes. Serve at once.

Serves 6

STEAMED TILAPIA AND RED CABBAGE

This low-cal, colorful dish is perfect for a quick supper or even an elegant dinner. The Asian pantry helps bring out a bit of fresh fixings. The chow mein noodles add a welcome crunch to the perfectly steamed fish. This is a great dish for people who love Oriental food and ginger but don't know if they like fish. The red peppers make it a particularly pretty dish, but it is still very nice without it. It reheats well in the microwave.

1 pound tilapia, grouper, or other thick
   fillets, cut into 1-inch pieces

1 teaspoon sesame oil

1 tablespoon olive or peanut oil

6 to 8 green onions, sliced into 1-inch
   pieces

2 garlic cloves, peeled and chopped

1 tablespoon chopped fresh ginger

2 carrots, cut into 1/8-inch matchsticks

1 red bell pepper, sliced (optional)

1 can sliced water chestnuts, drained

2 tablespoons dry sherry

1/2 cup fresh or canned chicken stock or
   broth

2 tablespoons soy sauce

1 tablespoon rice wine vinegar

1 teaspoon sugar

1/2 teaspoon red pepper flakes

2 tablespoons orange juice

4 cups shredded red cabbage

Salt

Freshly ground black pepper

1 cup chow mein noodles

In a large bowl, toss together the tilapia fillets and sesame oil. Set aside.
Heat the oil in a wok or frying pan until hot. Add the green onions, garlic, ginger, carrots, red bell pepper, and water chestnuts and stir-fry for about 2 minutes. Add the fish fillet pieces, the sherry, chicken stock, soy sauce, rice wine vinegar, sugar, and red pepper flakes. Cover and steam over medium heat about 5 minutes. Remove the fish and vegetables from the wok and set aside. Add the orange juice and shredded cabbage and stir-fry until the cabbage just begins to wilt. Place the cabbage on a platter and top with the fish, vegetables, and noodles. Season to taste with salt and pepper. Serve at once.

Serves 4

SMOKED TROUT POTATO SALAD WITH LEMON VINAIGRETTE

This lovely salad presents a variety of colors, flavors, and textures to delight the senses. It is a twist on the basic potato salad—low in calories, but rich in taste. Serve smoked trout salad as a first course or as the feature dish of a light lunch. If lettuce or spinach isn't available, then use a contrasting plate.

SMOKING FISH

There are many varieties of smokers from outdoors to indoors. When you have an abundance of fresh fish, it can be handy to smoke it all at one time. Do not be beguiled into thinking smoking preserves, however, in the manner that salting and curing does.

To smoke fish, place smoking chips in the bottom of your smoker. Place the fish on the rack of the smoker and cover tightly. Smoke for about 10 minutes per inch of thickness and check for doneness. The fish should register 150°F. to 170°F. on a meat thermometer. Cool, then wrap well and refrigerate for 3 or 4 days.

SALAD

6 small new potatoes

1½ to 2 pounds smoked trout, bluefish, or flounder (off the bone)

1 medium red onion, thinly sliced

2 medium tomatoes, cut in wedges, or equal amount of canned tomato wedges

1 cup thinly sliced cucumber

LEMON VINAIGRETTE

¼ cup finely chopped fresh basil (optional)

Juice of 1 lemon or ¼ cup lemon juice (page 85)

¼ cup white wine vinegar

2 tablespoons olive oil

Salt

Freshly ground black pepper

1 head of leaf lettuce or spinach (optional)

Scrub the potatoes, put them in boiling salted water, and simmer until done, 6 to 10 minutes. Set aside in the refrigerator to cool. Tear the trout into bite-size pieces and combine with the onion, tomato, and cucumber. When the potatoes are cool, chop them coarsely and add to the vegetables and trout.

Whisk together the basil, lemon juice, vinegar, olive oil, and salt and pepper to taste in a small bowl. Toss the salad with the vinaigrette and set in the refrigerator to chill for 30 minutes. Serve over leaf lettuce, spinach, or other greens if available.

Serves 4

ROAST CHICKEN AND ZUCCHINI WITH MOROCCAN MARINADE

I have always been partial to roast chicken. When it's rubbed with a marinade like this one, then roasted on top of vegetables, the cooking juices give the vegetables exquisite flavor. The marinade can be made ahead; after that, assembly takes just a few minutes. If you want to save yourself the step of turning the chicken midway, it is possible to put the chicken on top of the vegetables and not go back for over an hour; all you'll lose is crispness on the bottom of the chicken.

1 3-pound chicken	*2 onions, sliced*
½ cup Moroccan Marinade (page 114)	*6 zucchini, sliced*

Preheat the oven to 400°F. Grease a 13-inch roasting pan.

Rub the chicken with half of the marinade. In a mixing bowl, toss the onions and zucchini with the remaining marinade and spread them in the bottom of the roasting pan. Place the chicken, breast-side up, on top of the vegetables and cook 30 minutes. Remove from the oven, turn the chicken over, and bake 30 minutes more. Turn the chicken breast-side up once again and cook until golden brown all over and a meat thermometer inserted in the thigh registers 180°F., about 20 minutes longer. Let sit 10 minutes before carving.

Serves 4

CHICKEN BREASTS WITH DRIED APRICOTS AND CRANBERRIES

The only advance preparation required for this recipe is soaking the apricots and slicing the onion. The rest is just measuring seasonings and putting it all in a pan. Once that's done, an hour is yours—time to make the Dried Cranberry Pilaf (a perfect accompaniment, page 132) and a green salad and still be able to take a few minutes for yourself. That said, this is a delicious meal, far surpassing what you would expect from something so easy. (Dried cranberries are to fresh what raisins are to grapes. They are not easily substituted for each other.)

1½ cups dry white wine (regular or nonalcoholic)

1 cup dried apricots

6 chicken breasts, on the bone

1 large red onion, halved and sliced lengthwise

1 teaspoon ground coriander

1 teaspoon ground cumin

1 teaspoon paprika

½ teaspoon dry mustard

¼ teaspoon ground cinnamon

Salt

Freshly ground black pepper

½ cup dried cranberries

1 cup fresh or canned chicken stock or broth

Preheat the oven to 375°F.

In a saucepan, heat the wine just to the boiling point. Remove from the heat, add the apricots, and let soak for 10 minutes. Drain, reserving the wine and apricots separately.

In a large, heavy casserole, arrange the chicken pieces, skin-side up. Sprinkle the onion, coriander, cumin, paprika, dry mustard, cinnamon, salt, pepper, plumped apricots, and cranberries over the chicken. Combine the reserved wine and stock and pour over all. Cover the casserole tightly and bake until the chicken is very tender, 50 to 60 minutes.

Serves 6

NOTE: *One breast is one-half a chicken chest—improperly called "half a breast" by some. It has the bone and skin unless otherwise noted.*

MIDDLE EASTERN RATATOUILLE WITH GRILLED CHICKEN BREAST

We added Middle Eastern spices to a make-ahead ratatouille base that has become a freezer staple in my household. The ratatouille is exceptionally welcome when no fresh vegetables are available, and it "totes" very well too. I was delighted to find it enhanced grilled chicken breasts for an all-in-one light entrée that is full of color and flavor. It can all be made ahead, ready for the last-minute grilling or broiling of the breasts. And left-overs make a good ratatouille chicken salad. The ratatouille freezes well up to 4 months.

FREEZING TOMATOES
To freeze ripe tomatoes for use in cooked dishes, place, without touching each other, on a flat baking sheet in the freezer. When frozen, remove from the sheet and place in a storage container. Remove individually as needed. They may be peeled before freezing.

RATATOUILLE
3 tablespoons olive oil
2 large onions, chopped
4 garlic cloves, peeled and finely chopped
2 to 2½ pounds eggplant, peeled and cut into 1-inch cubes
1 28-ounce can Italian plum tomatoes
2 zucchini, cut into 1-inch cubes
2 yellow squash, cut into 1-inch cubes
½ teaspoon ground coriander
¼ teaspoon cayenne pepper
½ teaspoon ground cinnamon

¼ teaspoon ground cloves
Grated peel (no white attached) of 1 orange

MARINADE
¼ cup olive oil
¼ cup lemon juice
Salt
Freshly ground black pepper
½ teaspoon ground cumin
8 boneless skinless chicken breasts

Heat the oil in a large Dutch oven. Add the onions and garlic and cook, stirring constantly, until they begin to soften. Add the eggplant and cook, stirring, for 3 to 5 minutes. Add the tomatoes, zucchini, squash, coriander, cayenne, cinnamon, cloves, and orange peel. Bring to the boil, reduce the heat, and simmer over low heat for 50 to 60 minutes. Let stand at room temperature for up to an hour, refrigerate for up to 3 days, or freeze. Serve hot or at room temperature.

In a small mixing bowl, whisk together the oil, lemon juice, salt, pepper, and cumin. Pour over the chicken breasts and marinate ½ hour or overnight. When ready to serve, drain and grill over hot coals or under a hot broiler until just done, 3 to 4 minutes per side. Spoon a mound of the ratatouille onto each plate and top with a grilled breast.

Serves 6 to 8

CORNISH HENS WITH GINGER AND MARMALADE

The sweet, tangy flavor from the marmalade and ginger permeates the hens with incredible flavor. It's amazing that something so easy and found on your pantry shelf could be so good.

4 Cornish hens, about 1 to 1½ pounds each, backbone removed, flattened
Salt
Freshly ground black pepper
1 tablespoon chopped fresh ginger
½ cup orange marmalade

2 tablespoons Dijon mustard
2 tablespoons dry sherry
½ teaspoon red pepper flakes
½ cup fresh or canned chicken stock or broth

Preheat the oven to 400°F.

Place the Cornish hens breast-side up in a large shallow baking dish. Season to taste with salt and pepper. In a small skillet, mix together the ginger, marmalade, mustard, sherry, red pepper flakes, and chicken stock. Bring to the boil and cook for 1 minute. Pour evenly over the Cornish hens. Place in the oven and cook until a meat thermometer inserted into the thigh registers 180°F., about 1 hour. Serve a half or whole hen per person, topped with some of the sauce, and pass the remaining sauce separately.

Serves 4 to 6

TANGY CHICKEN BREASTS BAKED WITH BLACK BEAN SALSA

Easily sliced fresh zucchini and yellow squash and fresh cilantro combine with canned beans and tomato wedges to cut down on the time needed to put together this Southwestern-type one-dish meal, full of spices and zip. I hope you have a fresh lime. If not, use lemon juice. This dish freezes up to 3 months.

MARINADE
2 tablespoons fresh lime or lemon juice
1 tablespoon ground cumin
1 tablespoon ground coriander
½ teaspoon salt
½ teaspoon freshly ground black pepper
4 to 6 chicken breasts

SALSA
1 15-ounce can black beans, rinsed and
  drained
2 onions, cut into eighths

3 yellow squash, cut into 1-inch chunks,
  or 8 ounces frozen squash, defrosted
3 zucchini, cut into 1-inch chunks, or
  8 ounces frozen zucchini, defrosted
4 garlic cloves, peeled and sliced
1 14½-ounce can tomato wedges,
  drained, or 1 pound fresh tomatoes, cut
  into wedges
3 tablespoons coarsely chopped fresh
  cilantro
Salt
Freshly ground black pepper

Preheat the oven to 400°F.

In a bowl, combine the lime juice, cumin, coriander, salt, and pepper. Rub each breast with the marinade and set aside, 1 to 2 hours.

In a large bowl, toss together the black beans, onions, squash, zucchini, garlic, tomato wedges, and cilantro. Season to taste with salt and pepper. Place the bean mixture in a 13 × 9-inch baking pan and arrange the chicken breasts on top. Pour any extra marinade over the chicken and bake until the chicken is a nice golden brown and the vegetables are tender, about 1 hour.

Serves 4 to 6

CHICKEN CACCIATORE

FASTER DEFROSTING

I always have chicken in the freezer: boneless breasts, whole birds, and cut-up chickens as well. I've found it's better to freeze the cut-up birds than to defrost a whole chicken and then cut it into serving pieces; I cut up the chicken when I get home from the grocery store and freeze the pieces flat, then rewrap and store in the freezer.

The large amount of onions called for, almost equal to the tomatoes, adds a sweet, fruity taste and fragrance to this simple, classic Italian dish. For a more pronounced taste of Italy, add 2 teaspoons lightly crushed fennel seeds when sautéing the onions. A little sugar gives the tomatoes a boost in flavor. This dish freezes well.

1 3½- to 4-pound chicken, cut into
  8 pieces
Salt
Freshly ground black pepper
1 tablespoon oil, preferably olive
3 onions, sliced
4 garlic cloves, peeled and chopped
1 cup white wine (optional)

1 28-ounce can plum tomatoes, drained
  and juice reserved, coarsely chopped
1 teaspoon sugar
2 tablespoons chopped basil or oregano,
  preferably fresh
½ cup grated imported Parmesan cheese
4 cups cooked pasta, preferably spaghetti
  or vermicelli

Rub each piece of chicken with salt and pepper and set aside.

In a large skillet, heat the oil over medium-high heat. Add the chicken, skin-side down, and cook until golden brown on both sides, about 5 minutes per side. Remove the chicken from the pan, add the onions and garlic, and sauté until golden, about 10 minutes. Add the wine if using and chopped tomatoes with the sugar and place the chicken on top. If you are not using wine, add 1 cup of the reserved tomato liquid. Sprinkle with the basil, cover, and cook for 20 minutes. Remove the cover, toss the mixture gently, and continue cooking, uncovered, until most of the liquid has evaporated, about 15 minutes. Adjust the seasonings. Toss together the Parmesan and pasta. Serve the chicken and the sauce over the pasta.

Serves 4 to 6

NOTE: *I find that there is just the right amount of time to slice the onions and chop the garlic while the chicken is browning. I start the pasta water after the wine and tomatoes are added and the dish is simmering, then the water is boiling and I cook the pasta. When I cook pasta, I usually double the amount I need so that I'll have some for another meal or a pasta salad. It's not perfect, but is* much *better than canned spaghetti, for instance!*

CHINESE-STYLE CHICKEN

Here's another case where an Asian-inspired pantry makes two simple ingredients seem quite extraordinary. And yet all it requires is pulling a frozen chicken out of the freezer for an all-in-one dish. Slice fresh vegetables, such as zucchini, onions, or carrot and stir-fry quickly and toss with the pasta. To adapt to chicken pieces, bake them without the stock in a greased oven-proof pan until 180°F., about 45 minutes. Remove chicken, add the stock, bring to the boil, skim off some of the fat, and pour over the pasta.

1 tablespoon coriander seeds

1 tablespoon Szechuan peppercorns

1 tablespoon sesame seeds

1 teaspoon ground ginger

1 teaspoon Chinese five-spice powder

1 teaspoon ground mustard

2 green onions, chopped, or 1 small
    onion, chopped

2 garlic cloves, peeled and chopped

1 tablespoon chopped fresh ginger

1 tablespoon honey

3 tablespoons rice wine vinegar

3 tablespoons soy sauce

1 3½-pound chicken, rinsed and
    patted dry

½ cup fresh or canned chicken stock
    or broth

1 pound vermicelli or rotini

Preheat the oven to 400°F.

In a food processor or blender, combine the coriander seeds, Szechuan peppercorns, sesame seeds, ground ginger, five-spice powder, ground mustard, green onions, garlic, and fresh ginger. Process until coarsely chopped. Add the honey, vinegar, and soy sauce and mix until just combined. Rub the paste over the chicken and place in a roasting pan. Pour the chicken stock around the chicken and bake until golden and a meat thermometer registers 180°F. in the thigh, about 1 to 1¼ hours.

Meanwhile, bring a large pot of salted water to the boil. Add the pasta and cook according to package directions, just until al dente. Drain and place in a large serving bowl.

Transfer the roasted chicken to a cutting board or platter. Skim some of the fat off the pan juices, then scrape the pan with a wooden spoon to release any browned bits from the bottom and sides. Pour the pan juices over the pasta, toss well, and serve with the carved chicken.

Serves 4

MARYLAND FRIED CHICKEN

This recipe, from the collection of the Duchess of Windsor, uses very little fat, but satisfies like real fried chicken. To lower the fat count use broth or milk instead of cream in the sauce.

1 3-pound chicken, cut into 8 pieces
Salt
1 cup all-purpose flour
3 tablespoons solid vegetable shortening
  or oil

1 tablespoon butter
½ cup whipping cream, milk, or chicken
  stock or broth
1 cup chicken stock or broth from giblets
  (see Note)

Preheat the oven to 300°F.

Rub salt into the chicken pieces. Roll the chicken in the flour, shaking off the excess. Reserve the leftover flour.

Heat the shortening or oil over medium heat in a cast-iron skillet until hot. Add the butter. Place the chicken pieces in the skillet, skin-side down. Cover and cook 30 to 45 minutes, turning the frequently and letting them brown slowly on all sides. When browned, add 2 tablespoons water and place the covered skillet in the oven. Bake until the chicken is tender, about 30 minutes.

Remove the chicken to a plate. Pour off all but 2 tablespoons of the drippings. Stir in 2 tablespoons of the reserved flour. Add the cream, stock, and salt and pepper to taste. Stir constantly over low heat until thickened. Add chopped cooked giblets if desired.

Serves 4

NOTE: *Chop the neck and brown it in a little oil. Add 1 cup water and bring to the boil, scraping up the brown bits. Add 1 chopped celery stalk, 1 quartered onion, 1 small chopped carrot, 3 parsley sprigs, 1 bay leaf, and water to cover. Simmer for 1 hour. Add the giblets and simmer for 30 minutes. Strain. Chop the giblets and return to the stock if desired. Discard the other solids.*

JOZETTE'S BURGUNDIAN GODFATHER'S CHICKEN

Jozette Thiault's godfather was born in 1881 in a very rich region of France—la Bourgogne. He was a real gourmet and had many good recipes that her family was fond of, including this famous chicken. This dish is very good with small, peeled, boiled potatoes.

½ pound smoked bacon, cut into small pieces

1 cup pearl onions or 1 onion, sliced

1 3- to 3½-pound chicken, cut into serving pieces

1 teaspoon thyme

½ cup chopped fresh parsley

3 garlic cloves, peeled and chopped

1 teaspoon salt

1 teaspoon freshly ground black pepper

1½ to 2 cups red wine, preferably burgundy

8 to 10 dried black or shiitake mushrooms, soaked in warm water for 20 minutes and sliced or cut into quarters, or ¾ pound fresh mushrooms

¼ cup cognac, brandy, or Marc de Bourgogne

6 tablespoons (¾ stick) butter

3 pieces of bread, crust removed, cut into triangles

2 garlic cloves, peeled

2 tablespoons all-purpose flour

Arrange the bacon and onions in a Dutch oven. Put the chicken pieces on top, then the thyme, parsley, chopped garlic, salt, pepper, red wine, and ¼ cup water. Cover, bring to the boil, reduce the heat, and cook 40 minutes on medium-high heat. Turn the chicken pieces from time to time, taking care not to burn. Add the reconstituted mushrooms and cook 10 minutes longer. Add the cognac, brandy, or Marc de Bourgogne. Cook 5 to 7 minutes.

At the same time, heat 4 tablespoons of the butter in a skillet. Add the bread triangles and fry on each side until golden. Rub them with the whole garlic and set aside. Remove the chicken pieces and mushrooms from the pot and place in a deep serving dish; keep warm. Reserve the sauce.

Blend the remaining 2 tablespoons butter and the flour together to make a beurre manié. Blend a little of the sauce into the flour mixture, then return to the pot, bring to the boil, and cook until it thickens, stirring constantly. Arrange the croutons over the chicken and pour the thickened sauce over all.

Serves 6

TURKEY VEGETABLE LOAF

Delicious and very moist, this freezes well and provides vegetables when you haven't had time to stop by the greengrocer. Just about any vegetable will do, so you can use what's in the house. I really like the spaghetti sauce on top, but my editor, Pam Krauss, makes this and likes it better without.

GROUND TURKEY
Like a lot of people, I've taken to substituting ground turkey for ground beef in many recipes. It's handy to keep a pound or two frozen for impromptu cookouts or family meals; I especially like the turkey that comes already frozen in sausagelike 1 pound tubes.

2 pounds ground turkey
3 cups finely grated or chopped vegetables, any combination (carrots, zucchini, squash, mushrooms, green beans, peppers, onions)
½ cup cracker crumbs
1 cup breadcrumbs

2 eggs
2 tablespoons chopped fresh herbs, any combination (parsley, rosemary, thyme, basil, oregano)
1 teaspoon salt
1 teaspoon freshly ground black pepper
1 cup spaghetti sauce (optional)

Preheat the oven to 350°F.

In a large bowl, combine the ground turkey, vegetables, cracker crumbs, breadcrumbs, eggs, herbs, salt, and pepper. Press into two 9 × 5 × 3-inch loaf pans. Bake for 30 minutes, remove from the oven, and drain off any excess grease. Top with the spaghetti sauce if desired, return to the oven, and continue cooking until it registers 180°F., about 20 to 25 minutes. Remove from the oven and let rest 10 minutes before slicing.

Makes 2 loaves

TURKEY SAUSAGE WITH ITALIAN PLUM TOMATOES AND ANCHOVIES

This is best if it is allowed to sit, refrigerated, overnight and then served the next day. Everything just goes into one pot to simmer, making it particularly easy to make while preparing another meal. I had always used the fresh Italian sausage links, but once someone went to the store and came home with smoked turkey links, so I used them and I was pleased with them, too! Pork sausage links may also be substituted. I make this at the beach or mountains at the same time I'm cooking Chili sin Carne (page 33). That gives me several easily reheated meals particularly suited to lunch or simple suppers. Serve with pasta or plenty of good bread to sop up the wonderful sauce. This dish freezes for 3 months.

1 2-ounce can anchovy fillets

2 tablespoons olive oil

5 hot or smoked turkey sausage links, cut into ½-inch slices

1 28-ounce can Italian plum tomatoes

1 10-ounce can ripe olives, finely chopped

½ tablespoon finely chopped rosemary, preferably fresh

½ teaspoon anise seeds

1 large garlic clove, peeled and finely chopped

¼ cup vermouth

Pinch of sugar

Salt

Freshly ground black pepper

In a small bowl or with a mortar and pestle, mash the anchovies until they form a paste. Transfer to a medium saucepan and add the olive oil, sausage, tomatoes, olives, rosemary, anise seeds, and garlic. Bring to the boil over high heat. Reduce the heat, add the vermouth, sugar, salt, and pepper to taste, and simmer 30 to 45 minutes.

Serves 6

Pasta Dough ■ *Artichokes and Peas on Pasta* ■ *Pasta with Tuna, Tomatoes, and Garlic* ■ *Broccoli and Anchovy Pasta* ■ *Chickpeas and Pasta* ■ *Rotini with Garbanzo Beans, Sausage, and Herbs* ■ *Pasta with Lemon Butter* ■ *Pasta with Nuts and Cheese* ■ *Spaghetti with Creamy Tomato and Goat Cheese Sauce* ■ *Many Cheese and Spinach Lasagna* ■ *Vegetarian Lasagna*

5 PASTA AND LIGHT REPASTS

Pierre-Henri's Pasta Gratinée ■ *Old-Fashioned Vegetable "Mac N Cheese"* ■ *Mushroom Risotto* ■ *Sally's Seafood Risotto* ■ *Antipasto Pasta Salad* ■ *Quick and Easy Soufflé* ■ *Cheese-and-Whatever Enchilada* ■ *Duxelles Frittata with Three Cheeses* ■ *Broccoli-Cheese Pizza* ■ *Classic Pizza* ■ *Mushroom-Stuffed Egg Bake*

PASTA RIVALS potatoes and rice as the best conveyances for pantry staples. Part of the American cuisine, pasta is no longer just an Italian or Chinese starch. I generally cook twice as much pasta (and rice) as I need, refrigerating or freezing the remainder for another time. I do the same thing with spaghetti and marinara sauces. Anything leftover goes into a small freezer container ready to be popped out for one. Frequently, I make a casserole from the second batch of pasta to have on my freezer shelf. Needless to say, there is nothing wrong with keeping a good-quality spaghetti or marinara sauce on your pantry shelf, as well as an abundance of tomatoes of all sorts to accompany the pasta. I try to keep Parmigiano-Reggiano cheese in the freezer, too. A little grate of it enhances plain pasta with oil or butter—the variations are endless.

Eggs form the basis of many light suppers, and I grieve the disappearance of them from many menus out of cholesterol fear. They are, after all, a wonderful source of nutrition, and a wise pantry cook will rescue them from the doghouse and use them judiciously. A bit of canned peppers will zest up any egg dish, as will a spoonful of duxelles pulled from the freezer. Mushrooms have an affinity for eggs, and the old-fashioned Mushroom-Stuffed Egg Bake will prove popular on many occasions. A soufflé combined with a Pear and Prosciutto Salad would be a memorable meal. Omelets, frittatas, enchiladas, and pizzas will delight young and old alike, and can be made at home in the time it takes to have them delivered, so it's worthwhile to keep their makings in the cupboard.

PASTA DOUGH

Ideally, you have dry pasta on the shelf or fresh pasta from the store in the fridge or freezer. But if you want to dazzle sophisticated guests or charm children, it is actually quite simple to make your own. All you really need is flour and salt; the rest is easily varied. Any liquid can be substituted for the egg if no egg is at hand; try using spinach or beet cooking water rather than plain (Tip: 1 egg equals ¼ cup liquid). A pasta rolling machine gives the best results. It may be rolled by hand, of course, but it is a real challenge for the novice.

1 cup bread flour
1 large egg

1 teaspoon salt
1 to 3 tablespoons water

Mix together the flour, egg, and salt until you have a loose dough, adding water as necessary. Knead by hand on a floured board or place the ingredients in a food processor and process. The total kneading time will be a little more than 1 minute in the processor, 5 to 10 minutes by hand. Place the dough in a plastic bag and let it rest at room temperature for 30 minutes.

Feed the dough through a hand-cranked pasta machine at the widest setting. Repeat, reducing the width each time, stretching the dough until it is ⅛ inch thick, or as thick as you want it. The dough may be cut by hand or machine. To prevent sticking, dry on a rack or a floured surface for up to 30 minutes before cooking. The cut pasta may also be placed in a plastic bag and refrigerated up to 2 days or frozen to be cooked later. If frozen, place directly into a pot of boiling water and cook 3 to 5 minutes.

To cook, drop the fresh pasta into a large pot of rapidly boiling water for a very brief time, 2 to 3 minutes if very thin. The thinner and fresher the pasta, the shorter the cooking time. Dried pasta can take up to 10 minutes in boiling water. Taste to test doneness. When cooked it will be slightly resistant to the bite. Drain and serve with any of your favorite pasta sauces.

Makes ¾ pound; serves 4 to 6

ARTICHOKES AND PEAS ON PASTA

When I return home after a trip, often there is not a single fresh vegetable in the house. For such times I make sure there is always a package of frozen petite peas stashed away. And frozen artichoke hearts come in handy so often! I try to keep shrimp and country ham (vacuum sealed) on hand at all times, and when very flush I keep prosciutto, the aged Italian ham, in the refrigerator, hidden from the rest of the family. By combining these few ingredients, I can make this very alluring pasta dish from an empty vegetable bin.

¾ pound fettuccine or linguine
2 tablespoons olive oil
1 large onion, chopped
3 garlic cloves, peeled and finely chopped
4 slices country ham or prosciutto, finely chopped
2 to 3 tablespoons finely chopped fresh mint

2 6-ounce cans or jars artichoke hearts, drained, rinsed, and dried or equivalent frozen
1 cup frozen peas, thawed, or fresh peas
½ cup vermouth
1 cup heavy cream
Salt
Freshly ground black pepper
6 to 8 ounces cooked shrimp (optional)

Bring a large pot of salted water to the boil. Add the pasta and cook according to package directions, 6 to 8 minutes. Drain and keep warm.

Heat the olive oil in a large skillet. Add the onion and garlic and cook until soft, about 5 minutes. Add the ham or prosciutto, mint, artichoke hearts, and peas.

In another pan, bring the vermouth to the boil over high heat and reduce it to 2 tablespoons, about 3 minutes. Add the cream, return to the boil, and reduce by one-half, about 5 minutes. Stir the sauce into the vegetables and ham. Season to taste with salt and pepper. Add the shrimp if using and heat through. Add the cooked pasta, toss together until well coated and hot, and serve immediately.

Serves 6

PASTA WITH TUNA, TOMATOES, AND GARLIC

STORING GARLIC

Like most root vegetables, garlic keeps well if left in a cool, airy place (never store it in the refrigerator or in a plastic bag). But when I need just a few teaspoons, I find the chopped, oil-packed garlic in a jar works just fine. Unlike fresh garlic, garlic in oil must be stored in the refrigerator after the jar is opened or if you make your own.

Perhaps better than any other item, canned tuna epitomizes the bomb shelter basic. If you can't make this dish right out of the kitchen cabinet, you've probably just moved in! This pasta dish is easy to make, but your friends will think you spent a great deal of time preparing it. Linguine is traditional with this dish, but use any kind of pasta you have on hand.

¼ cup olive oil

1½ teaspoons finely chopped garlic

1½ cups canned imported Italian tomatoes, finely chopped, in their juice

1 to 1½ pounds pasta

3 6½-ounce cans tuna packed in oil

Salt

Freshly ground black pepper

1 tablespoon butter

3 tablespoons chopped fresh parsley (optional)

In a saucepan, heat the oil and garlic over medium heat just until the garlic turns to a light brown color, 1 or 2 minutes. Add the tomatoes and their juice to the garlic and oil. Stir and simmer for 20 to 25 minutes. While the tomatoes are simmering, cook the pasta in plenty of rapidly boiling, salted water according to package directions and drain well.

Drain the tuna thoroughly and crumble it with a fork. Turn off the heat when the tomatoes are done and stir in the tuna. Add salt and pepper to taste and the butter and mix well.

Toss with the cooked, drained pasta. Add the chopped parsley and toss again.

Serves 6

BROCCOLI AND ANCHOVY PASTA

This very delicious main course takes only the time it takes to cook the pasta. By then, everything else is ready. Broccoli is one of the vegetables I always try to keep on hand, both for its nutritional value and for its long shelf life, but you can certainly use frozen broccoli. Everything else comes from the pantry shelf. Canned anchovies are salty, so add salt only as necessary to suit your own palate. I cook and freeze pasta as well, defrosting it as needed in the microwave.

¼ cup olive oil
6 to 8 canned anchovy fillets
2 to 3 tablespoons capers, drained
Salt
Freshly ground black pepper

1 head of broccoli, florets cut off and
   blanched (reserve the stems for another
   use), or 1 package frozen chopped
   broccoli, thawed
½ pound of your favorite long pasta
   (linguine, capellini, etc.), cooked
½ cup grated imported Parmesan cheese

In a large skillet, heat the olive oil over medium-low heat. Add the anchovies and cook, stirring, until they begin to fall apart. Add the capers and salt and pepper to taste. Add the broccoli and cook until heated through, a minute or so.

Drain the cooked pasta well and toss with the olive oil mixture and the broccoli until well coated. Sprinkle with the cheese. Serve hot or at room temperature.

Serves 4

CHICKPEAS AND PASTA

SHAPED PASTA

Even if you like to make your own fresh pasta, for dishes that require small shaped pasta, dried is the only way to go. Lay in a supply of different flavors and shapes, such as orrecchiette, wagon wheels, rigatoni, penne, farfalle (bow ties) in whole wheat, or tricolors. They look very attractive stored in clear glass jars or canisters and it's more fun to vary the shapes you use, especially if you serve pasta often. The best shapes for freezing after cooking are those used in baked recipes—shells, ziti, manicotti, rotini, lasagna. Prepare the recipe and freeze before baking. To bake, thaw in the refrigerator overnight and proceed as the recipe directs.

When you combine the incomplete proteins of chickpeas with those of pasta you wind up with a complete protein. If you can find a green vegetable or a salad to keep it company, all the better. No one will realize that it is straight off your shelf. I vary this according to what's in the house. If you can't find chickpeas, by all means use a can of white beans, or even cook up some dried beans or peas. This dish can be made ahead and reheated.

½ cup oil, preferably olive

1 onion, chopped

2 garlic cloves, peeled and chopped

1 pound rotini or other tube pasta (tricolored is nice)

1 19-ounce can chickpeas or Great Northern beans

1 1-pound canned chopped tomatoes

¼ cup roughly chopped parsley, preferably fresh

1 teaspoon oregano or marjoram, preferably fresh

1 tablespoon fennel seeds

¼ teaspoon chili powder

Salt

Freshly ground black pepper

Heat enough of the oil to coat the bottom of a large frying pan. Add the onion and cook briefly until it starts to soften, 3 to 4 minutes. Add the garlic and continue to cook until both are soft but not brown, another minute or 2.

Meanwhile, bring a large pot of salted water to the boil. Add the pasta and cook according to package directions, 8 to 10 minutes, until al dente. Drain, rinse, and set aside. Drain the chickpeas or beans and rinse. Add any remaining oil to the pan. Add the pasta and chickpeas. Drain the tomatoes, reserving their juice. Add the tomatoes and add any juice from the tomatoes necessary to coat nicely. Add the parsley, oregano, fennel seed, chili powder, salt and pepper to taste. Add the pasta and toss over medium-high heat until warmed throughout. Serve hot.

Serves 4 to 6

ROTINI WITH GARBANZO BEANS, SAUSAGE, AND HERBS

This winning luncheon casserole was created one day when we were all hungry for a substantial meal but didn't have time to run to the grocery store. If you are watching your fat intake, use the new turkey sausage found in your supermarket's meat counter. We find it perfectly acceptable and it freezes, as does regular sausage.

1 tablespoon olive oil

1 pound hot Italian sausage, sliced into ½-inch chunks

1 onion, sliced

4 garlic cloves, peeled and chopped

1 tablespoon chopped fresh or dry rosemary

1 tablespoon chopped fresh or dry basil

1 tablespoon chopped fresh or dry oregano

2 tablespoons red wine vinegar

1 cup (4 ounces) rotini pasta, cooked according to package directions and drained

2 10-ounce packages frozen spinach, defrosted and squeezed dry

1 15-ounce can garbanzo beans, drained and rinsed

1 16-ounce can tomato wedges, drained

1 26-ounce jar spaghetti sauce

Salt

Freshly ground black pepper

1 cup grated imported Parmesan cheese

Preheat the oven to 350° F. Lightly grease a 9 × 13-inch baking pan. In a large skillet, heat the olive oil over medium heat. Add the sausage, onion, garlic, rosemary, basil, and oregano and cook, stirring, until the sausage is browned, about 8 to 10 minutes. Add the red wine vinegar. In a large bowl, toss together the pasta, spinach, beans, tomatoes, spaghetti sauce, and sausage mixture. Season to taste with salt and pepper. Pour into the greased pan, top with the Parmesan cheese, and bake until the cheese is browned and the casserole is bubbly, about 30 minutes.

Serves 8

PASTA WITH LEMON BUTTER

Pasta goes very well with lemon. Try spaghetti, fettuccine, penne, linguine, shells, rotini. To vary, toss in some tuna or cooked shrimp.

12 ounces pasta, any shape
1/4 cup (1/2 stick) butter
2 teaspoons finely grated lemon peel (no white attached)

2 tablespoons lemon juice
Salt
Freshly ground black pepper

Bring a large pot of salted water to the boil. Add the pasta and cook according to package directions, or until al dente. Drain

Meanwhile, melt the butter in a skillet over low heat or in the microwave. Stir in lemon peel and juice. Taste and season with salt and pepper. Toss with the pasta and serve hot.

Serves 4

PASTA WITH NUTS AND CHEESE

This makes an elegant meal with no effort. It is truly versatile, utilizing whatever variety of cheese, nuts, or pasta you happen to have in stock.

12 ounces vermicelli, fettuccine, or rotini
6 tablespoons olive oil or butter
2 garlic cloves, peeled and chopped
1/2 cup finely chopped walnuts, pecans, or pine nuts

1/3 cup grated imported Parmesan, blue, or cheddar cheese
3 tablespoons finely chopped fresh parsley (optional)

Bring a large pot of salted water to the boil. Add the pasta and cook according to package directions, or until al dente. Drain.

Meanwhile, heat the oil or butter in a small skillet. Add the garlic and cook until soft, about 1 minute. Add the nuts and sauté 2 minutes, until lightly toasted. Toss with the cheese, parsley if desired, and pasta, and serve hot.

Serves 4

SPAGHETTI WITH CREAMY TOMATO AND GOAT CHEESE SAUCE

If you have a canned tomato sauce you love on hand, you may use it, of course, but making your own from canned tomatoes is so good and so easy that there's no reason to buy ready-made. Canned Brie also works perfectly well in this dish.

3 tablespoons olive oil
2 garlic cloves, peeled and chopped
1 16-ounce can canned, chopped tomatoes
4 ounces goat cheese or Brie, in chunks
12 ounces spaghetti, cooked

2 tablespoons chopped fresh Italian
  flat-leaf parsley (optional)
Freshly ground black pepper

Heat the oil in a skillet over medium heat. Add the garlic and cook briefly, just until fragrant. Add the tomatoes and their liquid. Bring to the boil, reduce the heat, and simmer until reduced to a thick sauce, 10 to 15 minutes.

Add the cheese to the tomato sauce and stir over low heat until fairly smooth. Toss the hot pasta with the tomato sauce, parsley if using, and black pepper.

Serves 4

SOFT CHEESES

Sinfully creamy and delicate in flavor, most soft cheeses are more perishable than their harder counterparts, like cheddar or Parmesan. To prolong their shelf lives, keep soft cheeses tightly wrapped in the coldest part of your refrigerator. Some, including many goat cheeses, come packaged in airtight wrappings; don't open them until ready to use and then rewrap and refreeze after use. And consider keeping a canned Brie or Camembert, available in most grocery stores, on the shelf for those times when only a soft cheese will do. Saga blue also seems to last weeks in the refrigerator.

MANY CHEESE AND SPINACH LASAGNA

When the urge for lasagna strikes, I often find I don't have enough of only one cheese to feed a crowd, so I just grate or shred whatever I can find and it usually works out very well. My favorite is a combination of Parmesan, Gorgonzola, mozzarella, and fontina, but any mixture of semisoft cheeses would work. To vary, add ½ cup shredded, cooked ham or prosciutto.

½ cup (1 stick) butter

3 tablespoons all-purpose flour

1½ cups milk

1 12-ounce can chicken broth or stock

12 spinach lasagna noodles, cooked, drained, and kept in water

15 ounces ricotta or cottage cheese, drained

4 ounces grated imported Parmesan cheese

Salt

Freshly ground black pepper

½ cup chopped fresh parsley, thyme, or oregano (optional)

¾ pound combined grated or shredded cheese (Swiss, mozzarella, smoked mozzarella, Gorgonzola, Italian fontina, cheddar, goat, blue)

Preheat the oven to 350°F. Grease or butter a shallow 9 × 13-inch baking dish.

Melt the butter in a heavy saucepan. Add the flour, then stir in the milk and broth. Bring to the boil, stirring constantly. Spoon ½ cup of the sauce over the bottom of the baking dish. Remove 4 noodles from the water, dry, and arrange, slightly overlapping, on top of the sauce. In a bowl, mix together the ricotta and half of the Parmesan. Spread over the noodles. Season with salt and pepper and fresh herbs if available. Place another layer of noodles and top with half the combined cheeses and ½ cup of the sauce. Top with the remaining noodles, the rest of the cheese, the remaining sauce, and the remaining Parmesan. Bake until bubbly and browned, 50 to 60 minutes. Let stand for 5 or 10 minutes before cutting into squares and serving.

Serves 6 to 8

VEGETARIAN LASAGNA

This lasagna is so rich in flavor that the traditional meat sauce is not missed at all. It's a good way to get the kids to eat their vegetables but also dressy enough for company. The recipe calls for bell pepper and zucchini, but grated carrots would work well too; they could also be omitted if the vegetable bin is bare. Monterey Jack or even a mild cheddar can stand in for the mozzarella. It freezes for 2 months. Let thaw in the refrigerator overnight. Cover with foil and reheat at 350°F. for 30 minutes.

PRESERVING HERBS
When herbs are abundant in the late summer, layer them individually with oil in a small container to use as needed, shaking off the oil. They may also be frozen, wrapped tightly. Drying herbs is easy too, but less satisfactory as the herbs change their nature and it is hard to measure their potency.

1 tablespoon olive oil
2 onions, chopped
4 garlic cloves, peeled and chopped
1 cup mushrooms, sliced, or 2 4-ounce cans mushrooms, drained; or dried
1 red bell pepper, seeded and sliced (optional); or canned pimientos
2 zucchini, sliced (optional)
1 28-ounce can plum tomatoes, drained, juice reserved
1 6-ounce can tomato paste
2 tablespoons chopped fresh basil
2 tablespoons chopped fresh oregano
2 teaspoons fennel seeds, slightly crushed
Salt

Freshly ground black pepper
¼ cup red wine vinegar
2 cups lowfat cottage cheese or ricotta cheese, drained
2 10-ounce packages frozen chopped spinach, thawed and squeezed dry
1 10-ounce package frozen broccoli, thawed and chopped
3 tablespoons chopped fresh parsley
½ cup breadcrumbs
1 8-ounce package lasagna noodles, cooked according to package directions
1½ cups grated part-skim mozzarella cheese
¼ cup grated imported Parmesan cheese

Preheat the oven to 350°F. Lightly oil a 9 × 13 × 2-inch baking pan. In a large saucepan over medium heat, heat the olive oil until hot. Add the onions, garlic, mushrooms, and red bell pepper and zucchini if using and cook, stirring occasionally, until the vegetables are soft, about 10 minutes. Add the tomatoes, breaking them up with the back of a spoon. Bring to the boil, reduce the heat, and cook until most of the liquid has evaporated, about 8 minutes.

In a measuring cup, combine the tomato paste, 1 cup reserved tomato juice, basil, oregano, fennel seeds, salt and pepper to taste, and red wine vinegar. Stir into the vegetable mixture and cook over medium heat until thick and bubbly, about 30 minutes.

In a medium bowl, stir together the cottage cheese, spinach, broccoli, parsley, and breadcrumbs. Set aside. In the baking pan, place one layer of the noodles, one-third of the vegetable mixture, one-half of the cottage cheese mixture, and one-third of the mozzarella cheese. Repeat the layering process until all the mixtures have been used. Top with the Parmesan cheese. Bake until heated through and the top is lightly browned, 35 to 40 minutes. Let the lasagna rest 10 minutes before serving.

Serves 6 to 8

PIERRE-HENRI'S PASTA GRATINÉE

When Audrey and Pierre-Henri lived with me, he fixed this as a quick, last-minute meal. I was stunned at its ease—so much faster than macaroni and cheese and every bit as good, if not better! It is also lower in fat than the traditional macaroni and cheese, yet is a simple, very satisfying dish. Toss in some cubed ham or turkey breast for an easy main course.

1 pound spaghetti, fettuccine, or angel hair pasta
1½ cups grated Swiss, cheddar, or imported
   Parmesan cheese

Salt
Freshly ground black pepper

Preheat the oven to 375°F. Lightly oil a 9 × 13-inch baking pan.

Cook the pasta in plenty of rapidly boiling, salted water, according to package directions. Drain it and place it in the prepared baking pan. Sprinkle with the grated cheese and salt and pepper to taste. Bake until the cheese melts and begins to brown around the edges, 20 to 25 minutes.

Serves 6 to 8

OLD-FASHIONED VEGETABLE "MAC N CHEESE"

The addition of any leftover meat to this simple casserole will make it a satisfying one-dish meal. I've used many cheeses—even Saga blue. And I've also used frozen zucchini, squash, and broccoli.

2 tablespoons butter

2 onions, sliced

3 garlic cloves, peeled and finely chopped

2 zucchini (2 cups), cut into ½-inch cubes, or equivalent amount of broccoli florets, fresh or frozen

2 yellow squash, cut into ½-inch cubes

1 4½-ounce can pimiento, drained, or 1 roasted and peeled red pepper (page 106)

1 cup frozen peas, thawed

1 can tomato wedges, drained and chopped

4 ounces sharp cheddar or other strong-flavored cheese, grated

4 ounces grated imported Parmesan cheese

8 ounces pasta shells (or your favorite shape), cooked

3 tablespoons finely chopped fresh herbs (optional)

Salt

Freshly ground black pepper

Preheat the oven to 350°F. Lightly grease a 9 × 13-inch baking dish and set aside.

In a large skillet or Dutch oven, heat the butter. Add the onions and cook 3 to 5 minutes. Add the garlic and cook until soft, an additional 2 to 3 minutes. Add the zucchini, yellow squash, and pimiento and cook, stirring constantly, until almost soft, about 4 minutes. Add the peas, remove from the heat, and drain. Stir in the chopped tomato wedges. Combine the 2 cheeses in a small bowl. Toss the vegetable mixture with the pasta, stir in half the cheese and the herbs, and put into the baking dish. Season to taste with salt and pepper. Top with the remaining cheese and place in the oven. Bake until lightly browned, 15 to 20 minutes.

Serves 6 to 8

MUSHROOM RISOTTO

DRIED MUSHROOMS
There are wonderful dried mushrooms available, which can be soaked in boiling liquid and reconstituted in 20 minutes to toss into stir-fries, stews, sauces, or salads. Strain and save the soaking liquid and use it to flavor stocks, sauces, or grain dishes. Italian porcinis and French cèpes are meaty and flavorful but usually quite costly; also expensive, but delicious, Japanese shiitakes hold their shape well in sauces—look in Asian groceries for Chinese black mushrooms, which taste almost identical but cost far less.

Dried mushrooms add a wonderful flavor to rice from the shelf and Parmesan from the freezer.

2 ounces mixed dried mushrooms, such as porcini, black Chinese, shiitake, or button
4 cups boiling water
3 tablespoons butter
1 tablespoon olive oil

1 medium onion, finely chopped
1 pound Arborio or other short-grain rice
1 cup beef broth
1/3 cup grated imported Parmesan cheese
Salt
Freshly ground black pepper

Place the dried mushrooms in a bowl or glass measuring cup and cover with the boiling water. Soak for 30 minutes. Remove the plumped mushrooms with a slotted spoon. Squeeze the mushrooms to remove excess liquid. Strain and reserve the resulting liquid (stock). Roughly chop the mushrooms and set aside.

In a large skillet or casserole, heat the butter with the oil until it sings. Add the onion and mushrooms, sautéing for 2 to 3 minutes, until the onions are transparent but not browned. Add the rice and stir until thoroughly coated, 1 to 2 minutes.

Meanwhile, combine the mushroom stock with the beef broth. Stirring constantly, add 1/2 cup of the mixture to the pan and continue to stir over medium-high heat until all the liquid has been absorbed and the rice appears to be dry. Add another 1/2 cup of the liquid, following the same method. Over a 20-minute period, continue this procedure, being careful not to "drown" the rice. Stirring constantly, cook the risotto until it has reached a creamy consistency and is al dente.

When the risotto is done, stir in the Parmesan and season to taste with salt and pepper. Serve immediately.

Serves 4 to 6

SALLY'S SEAFOOD RISOTTO

This is a spectacular way to use canned seafood and rice. I love keeping short-grain rice on hand. In a pinch I've used Uncle Ben's. We've named it for apprentice Sally Young, as it was her first successful attempt at risotto.

3 tablespoons butter
1 tablespoon olive oil
1 medium onion, finely chopped
2 garlic cloves, peeled and finely chopped
1 pound Arborio or other short-grain rice
5 cups fresh or canned hot chicken stock or broth

⅓ cup grated imported Parmesan cheese
1 6-ounce can lump crabmeat, rinsed and drained, or equivalent amount of bay shrimp, rinsed, drained, and chopped
1½ tablespoons chopped fresh parsley
Salt
Freshly ground white pepper

In a large skillet or casserole, heat the butter and oil until it sings. Add the onion and garlic, sautéing until transparent but not browned. Add the rice and stir until coated well, 1 or 2 minutes. Stir in ½ cup of the hot broth. Stir constantly until all the liquid has been absorbed and the rice appears to be dry. Stir in another ½ cup of broth, continuing to stir as the liquid is absorbed.

Follow this method with the next 3 cups of broth, being careful not to "drown" the rice. The risotto should be kept over medium-high heat throughout the stir-cook process. This allows for even cooking and absorption of the liquid. After 20 minutes, all but 1 cup of the broth should be incorporated. Add the remaining cup, ¼ cup at a time, as needed. The risotto should be creamily bound together, neither dry nor runny, and is done when al dente—it has a little bite.

When the risotto is done, stir in the Parmesan, crab or shrimp, and parsley. Add salt and pepper to taste. Serve immediately.

Serves 6

NOTE: *Risotto is hard to reheat on top of the stove, but it does reheat well in the microwave.*

ANTIPASTO PASTA SALAD

An antipasto platter makes a wonderful appetizer but combining the traditional ingredients with pasta makes a marvelous main course or side dish for cold roast meats. If you favor rustic Italian fare you probably already have peperoncini peppers, olives, and sun-dried tomatoes on your shelves; smoked cheeses keep well and are different and unusual cocktail treats worth keeping around. Aged Gouda is incredible—like aged Parmesan it keeps a long time, freezes, and is a great addition to the pantry. This makes a perfect take-along meal for picnics or tailgating parties.

1 16-ounce box rotini or macaroni

4 garlic cloves, peeled and chopped

2 tablespoons coarse-grained mustard

$1/4$ cup red wine vinegar

$1/4$ cup balsamic vinegar

$1/4$ cup olive oil

Salt

Freshly ground black pepper to taste

1 cup sun-dried tomatoes, soaked in hot water for 10 minutes, drained, and chopped

1 cup smoked or aged Gouda or smoked mozzarella, cut into $1/2$-inch cubes

1 16-ounce can garbanzo beans, rinsed and drained

1 16-ounce can white beans, rinsed and drained

4 ounces hard salami, sliced thin

4 ounces ham, sliced thin

20 small peperoncini peppers

$1/2$ cup black olives, pitted and sliced

1 cup chopped fresh basil

$1/2$ to 1 cup grated imported Parmesan cheese

Cook the pasta according to package directions just until al dente. Drain and set aside in a large bowl.

In a small bowl, whisk together the garlic, mustard, red wine vinegar, balsamic vinegar, and olive oil. Season to taste with salt and pepper. Pour over the reserved pasta and toss to coat. Add the sun-dried tomatoes, Gouda cheese, garbanzo beans, white beans, salami, ham, peperoncini peppers, black olives, and basil. Toss and chill for at least 2 hours. Before serving, toss again and sprinkle with the Parmesan.

Serves 8

HOME SALUMERIA
Although antipasti in Italian signifies any dish served before the main course, both hot and cold, many of the foods commonly associated with an antipasto platter are dried, preserved, or marinated and keep extremely well in your pantry or refrigerator. If this is a favorite with your crowd, lay in a jar of peperoncini, roasted peppers, marinated mushrooms, and good olives (Italian gaetas are nice), plus a dried hard salami or two. Combined with some thinly sliced cheese and one or two vinegared vegetables (try fennel, beets, or artichoke hearts) or a lightly dressed lentil salad with lots of fresh parsley, you have a nearly instant spread.

CHEESE-AND-WHATEVER ENCHILADA

If you have some tortillas in the freezer, eggs, and a bit of cream, you can add leftover chili, canned tomato salsa, or whatever to come up with a dish kids and adults will love. You'll feel like a miracle worker!

8 extra large flour tortillas
12 large eggs
¼ cup heavy cream
½ pound Monterey Jack cheese, shredded

½ pound sharp cheddar cheese, shredded
1½ cups chili (page 33) or salsa
3 tablespoons finely chopped fresh cilantro (optional)

Preheat the oven to 350°F. Spray a 9 × 13-inch casserole with nonstick spray and line with some tortillas.

In a mixing bowl, combine the eggs and heavy cream and beat until just combined. Pour the egg mixture into a large, nonstick skillet and cook over medium heat, stirring constantly so the eggs do not stick or burn. When the eggs are firm but not set, pour them over the tortillas in the casserole. Cover the eggs with another layer of tortillas and sprinkle half of the Monterey Jack and cheddar cheeses over the tortillas. Spread with the chili or salsa and top with more tortillas. Sprinkle the remaining cheeses on top and sprinkle with the cilantro. Bake until the cheese is bubbly and the eggs are set, about 20 minutes.

Serves 10 to 12

SOUFFLES
When making a soufflé, so much depends on the dish size. If your soufflé is too runny when you start to serve it, don't panic! Serve the top and outside edges on individual plates and return the rest of the soufflé to the oven. Bring it out and dish up more as needed.

Small individual soufflés cook in much less time, just 10 to 15 minutes.

Don't throw any leftover soufflé away, even when it collapses. Serve it at room temperature or reheat it in the oven or microwave—it's still delicious a day or two later!

DUXELLES FRITTATA WITH THREE CHEESES

Duxelles from the freezer and bits of cheese combine with eggs for an exciting pantry meal. You can also sauté some finely chopped reconstituted shiitakes in a bit of butter, or go without mushrooms altogether.

1 tablespoon butter
6 eggs, mixed to a froth
½ cup Mushroom Duxelles (page 101)

¼ cup grated imported Parmesan cheese
¼ cup grated Swiss cheese
¼ cup grated sharp cheddar cheese

In a 9-inch nonstick pan, heat the butter until golden brown. Pour the eggs into the pan over medium-high heat and cook until set on the bottom, about 2 to 3 minutes. Spread the duxelles over the eggs and sprinkle with the Parmesan, Swiss, and cheddar cheeses. Run under the broiler until bubbly. Slide out of the pan onto a serving platter.

Serves 4

QUICK AND EASY SOUFFLÉ

When canned soup serves as the base rather than a more time-consuming white sauce, there is no reason not to serve a fabulous soufflé for a weeknight dinner!

1 tablespoon butter	*⅛ teaspoon cayenne pepper*
2 tablespoons breadcrumbs	*Freshly ground black pepper*
1 can cream of mushroom or cream of	*Salt*
chicken and broccoli soup	*4 egg yolks*
1 tablespoon Dijon mustard	*4 egg whites*
Pinch of ground nutmeg	*⅛ teaspoon cream of tartar*

Preheat the oven to 400°F. Remove the top rack from the oven and place a baking sheet on the bottom rack. Coat a 1½-quart soufflé dish with the butter and coat with breadcrumbs.

In a heavy 1-quart saucepan over medium heat, bring the soup, mustard, nutmeg, cayenne, and a couple of grinds of black pepper to the boil, stirring occasionally to keep from scorching. Remove from the heat, taste and adjust the seasoning, adding salt if necessary. Off the heat, whisk in the egg yolks one at a time.

In a large bowl, beat the egg whites and cream of tartar to stiff peaks. Stir a small portion of the beaten whites into the soup mixture to lighten it, then pour over the remaining whites and gently fold in. Pour into the prepared soufflé dish and place on the baking sheet in the bottom of the oven. Turn the oven temperature down to 375°F. and cook until the center is soft but not runny, 30 to 40 minutes. Remove from the oven and serve immediately.

Serves 4

CLASSIC PIZZA

I first ate this pizza with the smell of freshly picked grapes in the air, by the side of a Chianti vineyard. Pizza is a wonder and variations abound: sun-dried tomatoes and oil, chicken slices and your favorite barbecue sauce, tomato paste and mozzarella or Parmesan cheese, on and on.

1 tablespoon cornmeal
1½ packages active dry yeast
1 teaspoon sugar
1 cup warm water (105° F. to 115° F.)
2 tablespoons olive oil
1 teaspoon salt
3 cups bread flour

TOPPING
2 15½-ounce cans tomato wedges, drained and juice reserved
8 ounces mozzarella or Monterey Jack cheese
2 garlic cloves, peeled and chopped

Preheat the oven to 425°F. Lightly grease an 11 × 17–inch baking pan and sprinkle with the cornmeal.

Dissolve the yeast and sugar in the warm water. Place in a mixer bowl or food processor. Add the olive oil, salt, and enough of the flour, a cup at a time, to make a soft dough. Process 1 minute in food processor or knead 10 minutes by hand until the dough is elastic and smooth as a baby's bottom. Shape into a ball. Place in a greased plastic bag, turn to coat, and let rise until doubled in volume, about 1 hour. (The dough can be refrigerated for several hours at this point.)

When ready to use, roll out the dough in a rectangle and fit it into the baking pan. Arrange the tomato wedges over the pizza dough. Break the cheese into 1–inch chunks and scatter among the tomato wedges. Sprinkle with the garlic. Drizzle ½ cup tomato juice over the filling and sprinkle with the oregano, thyme, and pepper. Drizzle with the olive oil. Bake until the crust is slightly brown on the bottom, 12 to 15 minutes.

Makes one 12-inch round pizza

BROCCOLI-CHEESE PIZZA

This is a sophisticated pizza that is sure to please the younger crowd, too. I sometimes call this Good-for-You Pizza because of its whole wheat crust, vegetables, and negligible fat content. Like many yeast doughs, this one can be made in advance. When I know I'll be in a rush later I put the vegetables in separate containers and the dough in another, then I can roll out the dough and throw on the toppings just before baking.

DOUGH
1 package active dry yeast
1 cup warm water (105°F. to 115°F.)
1 tablespoon honey
1 tablespoon olive oil
2 cups whole wheat flour
1 cup bread flour
½ teaspoon salt
2 tablespoons cornmeal

8 ounces mozzarella cheese, grated
1 head of broccoli florets, lightly blanched,
or 2 boxes frozen broccoli, defrosted
1 small red onion, sliced
¼ cup thinly sliced basil leaves or ¼ cup
dried
Salt
Freshly ground black pepper

In a mixing bowl, dissolve the yeast in the warm water with the honey. Add the olive oil. Add 1½ cups whole wheat flour, the bread flour, and salt and stir to form a soft dough. Turn out onto a smooth surface and knead until smooth and elastic, adding more of the whole wheat flour as necessary to prevent sticking. Place in an oiled bag or bowl, seal or cover with plastic wrap, and let rise in a warm place until doubled in bulk. Alternately, put in the refrigerator until needed for up to 24 hours or freeze for up to 3 months.

Preheat the oven to 500°F. Sprinkle 2 cookie sheets or pizza pans with the cornmeal.

Divide the dough into 2 pieces. Roll each piece into a 12-inch round and place on a pan. Sprinkle each pizza with half the cheese, leaving a 1-inch border. Top with the broccoli and red onion. Sprinkle the pizza with the basil and season to taste with salt and pepper. Place on the bottom rack of the oven and bake 12 minutes or until lightly browned.

Makes 2 12-inch pizzas

MUSHROOM-STUFFED EGG BAKE

At first glance this recipe might sound too old-fashioned, but it is absolutely delicious. Every time I make it—it's my friend Savannah Walker's recipe—I'm begged for the recipe, just as I begged her for it. It makes a terrific brunch entrée or Sunday morning breakfast, especially when you're scraping the bottom of the barrel after a weekend of entertaining. It's best piping hot from the oven, but you can prepare the dish in advance, then pop it in the oven at the last minute.

6 hard-cooked eggs, peeled and halved

3 tablespoons butter, at room temperature

1 tablespoon Worcestershire sauce

2 cups finely chopped fresh, frozen, or canned mushrooms or $\frac{1}{2}$ cup Mushroom Duxelles (page 101), or 1 ounce dried mushrooms, plumped in water and drained

$\frac{1}{2}$ teaspoon salt

$\frac{1}{2}$ teaspoon cayenne pepper

S A U C E

4 tablespoons ($\frac{1}{2}$ stick) butter

3 tablespoons all-purpose flour

$1\frac{1}{2}$ cups milk

$\frac{1}{2}$ cup grated Swiss cheese

$\frac{1}{2}$ cup dry breadcrumbs

Preheat the oven to 350°F. Butter a 10- to 12-inch oval gratin dish.

Remove the yolks from the hard-cooked eggs and blend them with the butter, Worcestershire sauce, mushrooms, salt, and cayenne. Spoon the yolk mixture into the egg whites and place them in the buttered casserole. (The dish can be refrigerated up to 3 days at this point.)

To make the sauce, melt 3 tablespoons of the butter over low heat. Stir in the flour to make a roux and cook until lightly browned, about 4 minutes. Add the milk all at once and whisk until thickened and bubbly. Add the Swiss cheese and stir over low heat until melted; do not boil. (The sauce may be made several days in advance and refrigerated, covered with plastic wrap.)

Pour the sauce over the stuffed eggs. Melt the remaining tablespoon of butter in a small skillet or microwave. Toss the breadcrumbs with the butter, then sprinkle over the eggs. Bake 20 minutes and serve at once.

Serves 4

Mushroom Duxelles ■ White Sauce ■ Beurre Blanc Sauce ■ Sauce Brune
■ Oven-Roasted "Sun-Dried" Tomatoes ■ Mayonnaise ■ Red Pepper
Mayonnaise ■ Grilled Onion Relish ■ Pico de Gallo ■ Creamy Caesar

SAUCES AND ENHANCEMENTS

6

Dressing ■ Olive Paste ■ Cranberry Conserve ■ Spiced Honey ■ Raspberry
Yogurt Sauce ■ Beer and Grainy Mustard Marinade ■ Dipping Sauce
for Spring Rolls ■ Garlic Ginger Marinade ■ Moroccan Marinade or Rub ■
Hot Indian Spice ■ Peppered Lemon Rub ■ Candied Citrus Peel

MEALS ASSEMBLED from pantry ingredients are perhaps more dependent than any other kind on condiments and other enhancers to make them sing. Once you have the conveyor vehicles—eggs, pasta, rice, potatoes, or even chicken, fish, meat, or poultry—the sauces and enhancements are what pull it all over the top. Mayonnaise, pesto, marinades, spice mixtures or curry, and Mushroom Duxelles always add dash to a dish. I try to keep either the sauces themselves readily available, or the ingredients for them in my pantry. A mixture of mustards and vinegars can be combined with pantry ingredients to come up with creative new sauces and marinades; experimentation is imperative in the pantry kitchen.

This is perhaps the place to champion the cause of fresh herbs once again. They can bring the dreariest vegetable alive. They can brighten a sauce and make a dull meat sparkle. There is really no comparison between fresh and dried herbs, although obviously dried can be substituted when necessary. There is no hard and fast ratio for substitution. Drying generally concentrates an herb's flavor, but a fresh herb tastes much stronger than a dried one that has been sitting on a sunny shelf for years and years. The only thing to do is keep tasting.

It is my fervent hope that you can find a place for an herb garden even if it is only on a windowsill or a fire escape. I am fortunate that parsley, mint, and rosemary can grow all year long here, with the thyme sometimes keeping over, and the basil having to be planted anew each summer. (I have no luck with pot basil, alas, or cilantro.)

MUSHROOM DUXELLES

Mushrooms add a rich earthiness to foods that I love, but I find fresh cultivated mushrooms can get wizened and dessicated after a week or so in the refrigerator. Dried mushrooms (page 91) come to the rescue sometimes, but for an intense jolt of mushroom essence I prefer duxelles. Mushroom duxelles is an essential pantry flavoring ingredient that I make in large batches and freeze in small bags. This strongly flavored paste enhances meat, sauces, pâtés, soufflés, quiches, rice, pasta, soup, vegetables—everything but dessert! It freezes well up to 6 months. A small amount goes a long way. Tip: One pound mushrooms plus onions reduces to 2 cups.

¼ cup (½ stick) butter

1 pound mushrooms, cleaned and finely chopped

¼ cup finely chopped onion or shallots

2 garlic cloves, finely chopped

3 to 5 tablespoons finely chopped fresh parsley (optional)

Melt the butter in a large heavy frying pan over medium-low heat. Add the mushrooms, onion, and garlic and cook until the moisture has cooked out and is almost a paste, about 20 to 30 minutes. Add the parsley if desired. Store, covered, in the refrigerator for up to a week or freeze.

Makes 2 cups

NOTE: *You can chop the mushrooms in the food processor, but do not chop too finely; the duxelles should have some texture.*

WHITE SAUCE

A good white sauce is a true savior in times of stress. I make a milk stock first—if there are bits of mushroom, celery, or fresh vegetables around, I add them to the milk to increase the flavor. I put a white sauce over chicken, add Mushroom Duxelles (page 101) or cheese and use with pasta or top hard-cooked eggs, cauliflower, or broccoli with it, or layer with crepes, spinach, and just about any chopped or ground cooked meat.

4 cups milk
3 slices onion
1 bay leaf
2 slices carrot
6 peppercorns

5 tablespoons butter
5 tablespoons all-purpose flour
Salt
Freshly ground pepper, preferably white

Combine the milk, onion slices, bay leaf, carrot slices, and peppercorns in a saucepan and bring to the boil. Simmer 10 minutes. Strain and reserve the milk, discarding the vegetables.

Melt the butter in a heavy pan over medium heat. Stir in the flour and cook for a minute or so. Add the milk all at once and stir until boiling and thick, 3 to 4 minutes. Season to taste with salt and pepper as needed.

Makes 2½ cups

NOTE: *Prepare a basic white sauce using flour as the thickening agent and yogurt in place of the milk before adding yogurt to a dish to be baked. Cornstarch may be used if there is no flour.*

BEURRE BLANC SAUCE

A white butter sauce—also known as beurre blanc—is a wonderful emergency sauce that dresses up just about anything. Leftovers freeze or refrigerate well, and can be used to top reheated vegetables or tossed with rice, pasta, potatoes, and couscous. To reheat, whisk over low heat.

⅔ cup lemon juice
2 shallots, peeled and chopped
¾ pound (3 sticks) butter, cut into
    1- to 2-inch pieces

Salt
Freshly ground white pepper

Place the lemon juice and shallots in a saucepan and bring to the boil. Boil down until the liquid is reduced to 2 tablespoons, about 5 minutes, depending on the size of the pan. Whisk the butter, piece by piece, into the sauce over low heat. Taste for seasoning, strain if desired and serve warm.

Makes 1½ cups

Variations:

- Substitute a favorite wine vinegar, rice vinegar, white wine, red wine, lime juice, or orange juice for the lemon juice.
- Substitute ⅔ cup beer for the lemon juice. This is especially good with lobster or crab.
- Substitute 1 tablespoon finely chopped garlic for the shallots.
- Use ¼ cup fresh lemon juice plus ½ cup fresh or canned grapefruit juice. This is lovely with fish.
- Before whisking in the butter, add 2 tablespoons heavy cream and 1 teaspoon curry powder to the reduction. This is perfect over steamed scallops or shrimp.
- For a beurre rouge, substitute ½ cup red wine plus 2 tablespoons red wine vinegar. Whisk in ½ teaspoon tomato paste with the butter. After adding the butter, whisk in 2 tablespoons chopped chives and 1 tablespoon Dijon mustard.

SAUCE BRUNE

Cook any bits and pieces from the vegetable bin in butter, add flour and brown it, then thin with stock or broth and wine and you have a sauce fit for a king—or any meat. Try adding 2 sliced, cooked onions and a little wine vinegar for a Lyonnaise sauce. Or finish the sauce with dollops of butter. Combine brown sauce and any cooked meat to fill a crepe.

¼ cup (½ stick) butter
¼ cup finely chopped carrot
¼ cup finely chopped onion or shallots
¼ cup finely chopped bacon
¼ cup all-purpose flour
4 cups fresh or canned beef stock or broth
*   or roast juices*
½ cup white wine

1 teaspoon tomato paste
2 tablespoons mushroom stalks, peels, or
*   chopped mushrooms*
Bouquet garni of 2 parsley stalks, a
*   thyme sprig, and ½ bay leaf*
Salt
Freshly ground black pepper
½ cup Madeira or sherry

Melt the butter in a heavy saucepan; add the carrot, onion, and bacon and cook over low heat for about 10 minutes, uncovered, stirring occasionally. Add the flour and stir it over low heat for about 15 minutes to brown.

Add 3 cups of the stock, the wine, tomato paste, mushroom peelings, and the bouquet garni. Bring to the boil, reduce the heat, and simmer, uncovered, for 30 minutes. Skim off any froth that may rise to the surface. Strain and return to the pan. Discard the solids. Bring to the boil again.

Tilt the pan, skim off all the fat you can, and lower the heat so that the sauce will just simmer. Add half the reserved stock and bring slowly to the boil, skimming off any fat that comes to the surface. Simmer 20 minutes more, skim, add the remaining stock, boil again, and skim. Continue simmering until it reaches a coating consistency. Taste for seasoning and add salt and pepper. Strain once more into a clean saucepan. Meanwhile, bring the Madeira to the boil, reduce the heat, and boil until reduced by half, about 2 minutes. Add it to the sauce. Keep warm until ready to serve.

Makes 2½ cups

Variations:

- Whisk 1 teaspoon Dijon mustard into the finished stock.
- Add 2 tablespoons drained capers or peppercorns before simmering.
- Add 1 teaspoon brown sugar to the cooked vegetables and bacon. Cook 1 minute longer before browning the flour in the pan.
- Substitute 3½ cups stock plus ¼ cup Scotch.
- Sauce Poivrade: Substitute red wine for the white and wine vinegar for the Madeira and add 3 (or more) crushed peppercorns.

OVEN-ROASTED "SUN-DRIED" TOMATOES

OIL-PACKED VERSUS DRIED TOMATOES
Dried tomatoes come in many forms. You can make your own or purchase them. They can be chopped (and used as you would crumbled bacon), whole, halved, or sliced. They are sold dried, plumped, and packed in oil or just dried. For some recipes the dried need to be plumped in boiling liquid (usually water) for 30 seconds or so and then packed-in-oil sliced. Use oven-dried or sun-dried tomatoes on pizza with cheese (mozzarella, goat cheese, Monterey Jack, etc.) or tossed with pasta.

This is one way to guarantee good, flavorful tomatoes year-round. When tomatoes are abundant, buy a case or so of plum or Roma tomatoes and dry them yourself. The results are to tomatoes what raisins are to grapes, and they are so delicious I've been known to eat them as is. They get drier and harder as time goes on. To reconstitute, cover with boiling water and let sit until softened. The soaking liquid may be used to flavor soups, rice dishes, and dressings if desired.

Preheat the oven to the lowest setting, below 200°F.

Slice Italian-style (Roma or plum) tomatoes in half lengthwise. Scoop out the seeds with your fingers. Spray your oven racks with nonstick cooking spray. Place the tomatoes, cut-side down, directly on the oven racks and let them dry out for 12 to 15 hours. Place a pan or aluminum foil beneath the racks to catch the drippings. Remove from the oven and cool. When cool, store in an airtight container at room temperature or freeze. They will keep indefinitely.

MAYONNAISE

Many's the time I had a craving for a good old tuna sandwich on toast, only to find the mayo is gone. I make up a quick batch of mayonnaise in less than the time it would take to get to the store and back.

2 whole eggs, at room temperature
Salt
Freshly ground black pepper
⅛ teaspoon Dijon mustard

½ to 1 cup oil, at room temperature or
    warmer
2 to 3 tablespoons lemon juice

In a small bowl, using a small whisk, beat the eggs and ⅛ teaspoon each of salt, pepper, and mustard until thick and sticky. Add 2 tablespoons of the oil, a little at a time, then stir in 1 teaspoon of the lemon juice. Add the remaining oil, 1 tablespoon at a time, beating after each addition until it is absorbed. When all the oil has been absorbed, add the remaining lemon juice to taste and extra salt and pepper as necessary.

Makes 1¼ to 1¾ cups

RED PEPPER MAYONNAISE

Enhanced with roasted red bell peppers, this is a full, rich-flavored cold sauce to serve with roasted or grilled meats or poultry. It is great on sandwiches, too. Store in the refrigerator up to 2 weeks.

2 cups mayonnaise
2 fresh or jarred roasted red bell peppers
    (see sidebar)
6 tablespoons finely chopped fresh basil

1 tablespoon lemon juice
Salt
Freshly ground black pepper

In a food processor or blender, puree the mayonnaise, peppers, basil, and lemon juice. Season to taste with salt and pepper.

Makes 2½ cups

GRILLED ONION RELISH

YEAR-ROUND SWEET ONIONS

Vidalia, Texas Sweet, and Walla Walla onions compete for sweetness nearly year-round. While the growing season for sweet, mild onions is brief, improved cold-storage techniques have stretched the time they are available in supermarkets. If you, like me, buy them by the 25-pound sack, careful storage will allow you to feast on Vidalias all year. Try the panty hose technique of knotting onions in a pair of clean hose, leaving an inch or so between each. The Texas Sweet people sent me a specially designed mesh tubing! Either method keeps the onions from rubbing together and possibly rotting at the point of contact.

This versatile, all-purpose relish works as an accompaniment to meats, grilled seafood, green vegetables, or as a spread for crackers. Grilling the onions gives them a characteristic smoky flavor; if this is not feasible, baking them in the oven is a perfectly acceptable alternative. If available, try using the Georgia sweet Vidalia onion. When grilled, the natural sugars in the onion caramelize, adding a whole new dimension to the taste. If using the Vidalia onion, be sure to omit the sugar. The onion's mellow flavor is sweet enough. Fresh fennel puts this over the top, but is, of course, expendable. This relish will last 2 weeks in the refrigerator.

2 tablespoons olive oil

2 tablespoons Dijon mustard

2 tablespoons fresh rosemary (not chopped)

3 large red onions, peeled and cut in half or quarters, root intact

3 large yellow onions, peeled and cut in half or quarters, root intact

1 teaspoon fennel seeds

½ cup chopped fennel bulb or California anise

¼ cup balsamic vinegar

1 teaspoon sugar (optional)

Salt

Freshly ground black pepper

½ cup toasted and chopped pecans (optional)

Mix the olive oil, Dijon, and rosemary and brush on the onions. Place the onions on a grill over medium-hot coals until the onions begin to soften and char slightly, about 20 minutes, turning every 5 minutes or so. Alternately, the onions may be sliced and baked in a single layer on a baking sheet in a pre-heated 400°F. oven about 20 to 25 minutes, turning once. Coarsely chop the onions and put them in a bowl. Add the fennel seeds, chopped fennel, balsamic vinegar, and sugar if using. Season to taste with salt and pepper. Add the pecans if desired. Cover and refrigerate 4 hours before serving to allow the flavors to develop fully. Serve at room temperature.

Makes 4 cups

PICO DE GALLO

This is a simple but very tasty salsa-type dip or topping. Be sure to do the chopping by hand, as a food processor tends to turn the ingredients to mush. It will keep for 3 to 4 days in the refrigerator. If all you have on hand are canned tomatoes, use them—what you'll end up with is a saucier sauce!

3 plum tomatoes, coarsely chopped
½ red onion, finely chopped
4 green onions, chopped
1 carrot, peeled and shredded (optional)
½ cup black olives, chopped (optional)
2 jalapeño peppers, seeded and chopped
6 garlic cloves, peeled and chopped

1 tablespoon chopped fresh parsley
2 tablespoons chopped fresh cilantro
¼ cup fresh lime juice
¼ cup grated lime peel (no white
  attached)
Salt
Freshly ground black pepper

In a large bowl, mix together the tomatoes, red onion, green onions, carrot, olives, jalapeño peppers, garlic, parsley, cilantro, lime juice, lime peel, and salt and pepper to taste. Let sit 2 hours before serving to allow the flavors to marry..

Makes 2 cups

Variation:
Stir in a 15-ounce can black beans or black-eyed peas, rinsed and drained.

CREAMY CAESAR DRESSING

This can be used as a dressing for an escarole salad with croutons, a dip for crudités, or as a topping for canned escargots (bake just until the snails are heated through, about 7 minutes at 350°F.). The egg yolks make it rich and creamy, but if you're fearful your eggs are not free of salmonella contamination, choose another recipe.

2 egg yolks

2 tablespoons Dijon mustard

8 anchovy fillets

6 garlic cloves, peeled and finely chopped

¼ cup red wine vinegar

2 tablespoons lemon juice

2 cups olive oil

1 cup grated imported Parmesan cheese

Salt

Freshly grated black pepper

Sugar

In a food processor or blender, combine the egg yolks, mustard, anchovies, garlic, vinegar, and lemon juice until smooth. In a slow, steady stream, add the olive oil, processing until the mixture is thick and creamy. Stir in the grated cheese. Season to taste with salt, pepper, and sugar. Refrigerate for 1 hour before using.

Makes 3 cups

OLIVE PASTE

FLAVORFUL OLIVES

Whenever possible buy a well-flavored olive and avoid the rubbery canned type. I particularly love the oil- and herb-packed Niçoise olives as well as the brine-packed Greek ones. I love seeing the array of olives available in California and Europe. Once opened I keep olives in the refrigerator.

This paste is a great way to perk up soups or stews. You can spread it on crackers or French bread, add it to pasta or deviled eggs, or mix it with a vinaigrette to create a unique salad dressing or marinade for steamed vegetables. Its uses are unlimited and it lasts for 6 months in the refrigerator.

1 cup Kalamata or mixed green and
    black olives

1 medium onion, chopped

3 tablespoons capers, rinsed

1 tablespoon chopped fresh oregano or
    1½ teaspoons dried

3 tablespoons olive oil

2 tablespoons red wine vinegar

Grated peel (no white attached) of 1
    lemon

½ teaspoon freshly ground black pepper,
    or to taste

Place the olives in a colander and rinse very well under cold running water. Remove the pits from the olives and discard. In the bowl of a food processor, combine the pitted olives, onion, capers, oregano, olive oil, vinegar, and lemon peel. Process to a spreading consistency. Season to taste with the pepper and store in a small jar in the refrigerator.

Makes 1 cup

CRANBERRY CONSERVE

We always try to keep this conserve on hand throughout the holidays. This is an excellent condiment for the holiday turkey or a simple pork tenderloin. Be sure to use a plastic spoon when stirring; a wooden spoon will absorb the cranberry color. This can also be mixed with cream cheese and leftover chopped turkey and spooned into little pastry cups for a quick and easy cocktail munchie. It freezes 2 to 3 months.

1 pound cranberries (about 4 cups)
1½ cups orange juice
3 cups sugar
1 cup crushed pineapple, drained
½ cup raisins or currants

2 oranges, peeled, seeded, and cut into
*   wedges or sections*
½ cup chopped walnuts

Combine the cranberries and orange juice in a 3-quart heavy saucepan. Bring to the boil over moderately high heat and cook 6 to 8 minutes, or until the berries begin to pop and are tender. Stir in the sugar, pineapple, raisins, and oranges. Reduce heat to low and simmer, uncovered, stirring occasionally, for 1 hour, or until thick and jamlike. Stir in the walnuts. Store in the refrigerator for up to a month or freeze.

Makes 4 cups

SPICED HONEY

Awesome! This sweet spread makes everything from hot tea to scones, even breakfast toast, taste better. It makes a nice holiday gift but also picks up a pantry breakfast.

1 cup honey
1 or 2 pieces of candied ginger
6 whole cloves
2 allspice berries

1 cinnamon stick
2-inch strip of orange peel (no white attached)

In a jar, combine the honey, ginger, cloves, allspice berries, cinnamon stick, and orange peel. Cover and let sit at room temperature for 7 days to develop the flavor. Strain and place in a decorative jar.

Makes 1 cup

RASPBERRY YOGURT SAUCE

An absolutely delicious, low-calorie, lowfat, last-minute sauce, Raspberry Yogurt Sauce is an easy quick topping that can be multiplied up and made ahead. Freeze in individual pint-size freezer bags and defrost as needed.

1 cup lowfat Yogurt Cheese (page 19)
1 12-ounce package frozen raspberries

2 teaspoons lemon juice
2 tablespoons sugar

In a blender or food processor, mix the Yogurt Cheese, raspberries, lemon juice, and sugar until smooth. Strain if desired. Refrigerate until needed, up to 2 days.

Makes 1½ cups

BEER AND GRAINY MUSTARD MARINADE

This is a simple, throw-together marinade that is very good for red meats such as beef or lamb. The alcohol in the beer in no way affects the flavor of this marinade, so a nonalcoholic variety can easily be used or 1½ cups tomato or vegetable juice could also be substituted. If you don't have a coarse-grained mustard on hand, add 1 tablespoon whole mustard seed instead. This marinade will last 1 week in the refrigerator.

1 12-ounce bottle beer or 1½ cups
  tomato or vegetable juice
¼ cup Dijon country or grainy-style
  mustard
2 tablespoons red wine vinegar
2 tablespoons brown sugar

2 teaspoons prepared horseradish
2 bay leaves, crumbled
1 teaspoon Tabasco sauce, or more to
  taste
Freshly ground black pepper

In a 1-quart bowl, mix together the beer, mustard, vinegar, brown sugar, horseradish, bay leaves, Tabasco, and pepper to taste. Stir together until the mixture is thoroughly combined. Store, tightly covered, in the refrigerator.

Makes 2 cups

MUSTARDS
Making your own mustard? If you're caught short you can either add water and vinegar to powdered mustard or boil seeds in vinegar and blenderize. Keep Dijon on hand, and add flavors as you want them—grainy, ballpark (yellow), and horseradish are a few of the varieties you might want to add to the pantry. They're great for sauces, marinades, and, of course, sandwiches.

DIPPING SAUCE FOR SPRING ROLLS

This sauce is a wonderful alternative to plain Chinese mustard, soy sauce, or sweet-and-sour sauce for spring rolls or egg rolls. It lasts indefinitely in the refrigerator.

½ cup rice or rice wine vinegar
¼ cup soy sauce
1½ teaspoons sesame oil

1½ teaspoons hot chili oil or hot chili
  sesame oil

In a small bowl, combine the vinegar, soy sauce, sesame oil, and hot chili oil or hot chili sesame oil. Mix thoroughly and store, tightly covered, in the refrigerator. Serve with spring rolls.

Makes 1 cup

GARLIC GINGER MARINADE

This is a fairly thick marinade with generous amounts of garlic, ginger, green onions, and sesame seeds—all basics in any Asian pantry. The marinade is great for less expensive cuts of beef or pork because the rice wine vinegar acts as a tenderizer. This marinade can also be brought to the boil, simmered briefly, and served with the meat as a sauce. For a more pronounced Oriental flavor, toast the sesame seeds until lightly browned, about 2 to 3 minutes at 375°F. The marinade will last 1 week in the refrigerator.

6 garlic cloves, peeled and chopped

1 tablespoon freshly grated ginger

2 tablespoons sugar

2 tablespoons peanut oil (optional)

6 green onions, green and white parts, chopped

1 teaspoon red pepper flakes

4 teaspoons rice wine or white wine vinegar

2 tablespoons sesame seeds

2 tablespoons soy sauce

1 teaspoon sesame oil

In a 1-quart bowl, mix together the garlic, ginger, sugar, peanut oil if using, green onions, red pepper flakes, rice wine vinegar, sesame seeds, soy sauce if using, and sesame oil. Stir until thoroughly blended.

Makes 2 cups

SOY SAUCE
Whether or not you have a full-scale Asian pantry, you should have soy sauce around to make dressings and dipping sauces and to flavor stir-fries. Tamari soy sauces are strong flavored and thick, while Chinese are thinner but can be bitter to western palates. Japanese soy sauces are the most readily available and come in a thick, syrupy dark form or the lighter more familiar version (it's what you see filling the bottles at sushi bars). Don't confuse the latter with "lite" or low-sodium soy sauces; these generally have poor flavor. If you wish to cut down on sodium, simply thin your regular soy sauce with water.

MOROCCAN MARINADE OR RUB

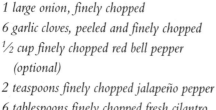

This robustly seasoned blend is good on chicken, fish, or pork, tossed with pasta or white beans, dropped in soup—any time you want a burst of flavor. Store in the refrigerator up to 2 weeks.

1 large onion, finely chopped
6 garlic cloves, peeled and finely chopped
½ cup finely chopped red bell pepper (optional)
2 teaspoons finely chopped jalapeño pepper
6 tablespoons finely chopped fresh cilantro
¼ cup finely chopped fresh parsley
Juice of 3 lemons, strained
Grated peel (no white attached) of 2 lemons

Grated peel (no white attached) of 2 oranges
1 teaspoon turmeric
2 teaspoons saffron
1 teaspoon ground coriander
1 teaspoon paprika
1 teaspoon ground cinnamon
2 teaspoons cumin seeds
Salt
Freshly ground black pepper

In a large bowl, combine the onion, garlic, red bell pepper if using, jalapeño pepper, cilantro, parsley, lemon juice, lemon and orange peels, turmeric, saffron, coriander, paprika, cinnamon, and cumin seeds. Season to taste with salt and pepper.

Makes 1½ cups

DRIED CITRUS PEEL
Having frozen lemon or lime juice in the freezer isn't much help when I want to add the extra citrus punch that grated zest adds to a dish. A good habit is to always grate or chop the zest of a citrus fruit before you juice it, then wrap well and freeze. As an alternative, I discovered a superior dried orange peel in a Middle Eastern spice shop, and now I keep a small jar of it to reconstitute and stir into marinades, sauces, and baked goods. Steep in boiling water, then drain and press dry in a dish towel.

HOT INDIAN SPICE

Rodney and Steve Farmer, my apprentices, didn't have much experience with Indian cooking. They sat down and read Julie Sahni's book *Classic Indian Cooking,* then made up this zesty version of garam masala. I keep it in a zip-type plastic bag in the freezer. It's a good substitute for curry powder.

2 tablespoons ground cardamom

1 tablespoon ground cinnamon

1 tablespoon whole cloves

$\frac{1}{4}$ cup black peppercorns

$\frac{1}{2}$ cup cumin seeds

$\frac{1}{2}$ cup coriander seeds

Combine all the ingredients in a food processor or blender and process until the mixture is a fine powder. Store in an airtight container in a cool place.

Makes 1$\frac{1}{2}$ cups

PEPPERED LEMON RUB

This is a very quick and easy dry rub for grilled or baked beef or poultry. It develops a nice crust as it cooks and adds a bit of a zing when you bite into it. The lemon brings a subtle tartness but the flavor is much brighter than any store-bought lemon pepper. Green peppercorns are available dried as well as brine-packed.

3 tablespoons freshly cracked black peppercorns

1 tablespoon freshly cracked dried green
   peppercorns (optional)

1 tablespoon freshly ground white pepper

$\frac{1}{2}$ teaspoon cayenne pepper

$\frac{1}{2}$ teaspoon red pepper flakes

1 tablespoon grated lemon peel (no white
   attached)

In a small bowl, combine the black peppercorns, green peppercorns if using, white pepper, cayenne, red pepper flakes, and lemon peel. Store in a tightly covered container for up to a week or freeze.

Makes $\frac{1}{2}$ cup

CANDIED CITRUS PEEL

Alike the way of the bitterness of the thick rinds contrasts with the crusty sugariness of its sweet coating. When I'm trying to avoid fats and sweets but can't completely avoid temptation, I make up a batch of these tangy–sweet rinds to snack on in the mountains. They tote and store easily, and I feel virtuous using the rind as well as the fruit!

10 navel oranges
5 grapefruit or 14 lemons

6 cups sugar
Chocolate Dipping Sauce (recipe follows), optional

With a sharp knife, make 6 lengthwise incisions (top to bottom) in the peel of the fruit. Separate the fruit from the peel, reserving the fruit for another use. Put the peel into a medium-size pot of boiling water, return to the boil, let boil for 30 seconds, drain, and rinse under cold water. Repeat 2 more times to remove bitterness.

Return the peel to the pot, add 4 cups of the sugar and 2 cups of water. Bring to a slow boil and simmer gently for about 1 to 1½ hours, stirring occasionally. With tongs or a fork, remove the peel from the syrup and drain the pieces, skin-side up, on a wire rack. Let dry for 1 hour.

In a medium bowl, toss the peel with the remaining 2 cups sugar until evenly coated. Place the peel on a baking sheet lined with wax paper. Set in a cool, dry place overnight to harden. Store in tightly fitted jars for up to 2 weeks.

The peel can be dipped in Chocolate Dipping Sauce if desired. Let cool in the refrigerator until the chocolate is set, about 1 hour.

Makes 90 to 144 pieces

CHOCOLATE DIPPING SAUCE

4 ounces semisweet chocolate
2 ounces unsweetened chocolate

1 teaspoon vegetable oil

Melt the chocolate slowly over low heat. Add the oil and stir briskly until shiny. Dip the dried, sugar–coated peel in the chocolate and place on wax paper until the chocolate is set.

Spinach "Bouillabaisse ■ Hot Carrots with Pine Nuts ■ Honey Gingered Carrots ■ Company Cabbage ■ Spicy Brussels Sprouts ■ Braised Celery ■ Sautéed Mushrooms ■ Mushrooms à la Grecque ■ Broccoli Spears Drenched with Garlic ■ Pepper Mélange ■ Gingered Beets with Yogurt Dressing ■ Cauliflower Niçoise ■ Potato Flowers ■ Crispy Brown Potatoes ■ Mashed Potatoes ■ Oven-Fried Sweet Potato Chips ■ Dried Cranberry Pilaf

7
SIDE DISHES AND SALADS

■ Southern Browned Rice ■ Bert's Forty-Carat Quinoa ■ Oven-Baked Onion Rice ■ Rice with Dried Fruit ■ Couscous Pilaf ■ Pecan Dressing ■ Orzo with Lemon, Capers, and Herbs ■ Potato Gnocchi with Pesto ■ Desperation Pasta Salad ■ Spicy Black-Eyed Pea and Jicama Salad ■ Warm Salad of Broccoli with Red Pepper, Olives, and Feta ■ New Potato and Red Onion Salad ■ Ribbon Slaw ■ Pear and Prosciutto Salad

IT IS NATURAL TO look to the well-stocked pantry for vegetable and side dishes, as so many of us were reared on meals served up with frozen succotash or canned beans. And of course potatoes, rice, grains, and beans, the basis of endless side dishes, are the workhorses of the pantry. But by buying fresh vegetables judiciously and combining them with pantry staples, it is possible to create salads, vegetable dishes, and other accompaniments that add sparkle to any meal.

The trick is to purchase vegetables of various staying powers. Some, like cabbage, that keep longer, can be used toward the end of the shopping cycle. Rank your vegetables mentally for perishability, or better yet, make yourself a note for the refrigerator door, reminding you to use the zucchini before Tuesday. Salads are not what we usually think of when we think of pantry cooking, but in fact it is quite easy to ensure you'll have ingredients for salads around, no matter how long it's been since you've shopped. When I was growing up my working mother could only shop once a week. We would start off the week with lettuce, well washed, wrapped, and kept in the bottom of the refrigerator. When in season, tomatoes would ripen on the windowsill, and cucumbers were marinated in plain vinegar. Later in the week would come slaws, potato salads, carrots with raisins, and finally canned beets, mandarin oranges, and canned beans, all cleverly disguised to make us think we were eating something fresh. Many vegetables, especially root cellar denizens, require no refrigeration and are almost endlessly adaptable.

Alternate fresh ingredients with frozen, canned, and dried. Neither are all bad, gourmets to the contrary. In fact, frozen English green peas are frequently superior to fresh. (And canned English peas ought to be avoided.) Frozen broccoli is very handy, although fresh keeps so well that I generally try to keep some on hand. Whole leaf frozen spinach discourages me because so much is stem; the chopped allows me to pretend more is leaf than stem, so I prefer it. Like frozen cauliflower and Brussels sprouts, it is best defrosted, then reheated, rather than "cooked." I use frozen corn, butter beans, black-eyed peas, and whiteacre peas, preferably those I put up myself.

Canned vegetables vary considerably in quality, but there are many I cannot do without. I prefer a juicy canned tomato to a pale pink fresh one, and I use a good many canned Italian plum tomatoes. (Good tomatoes come in long-life boxes as well.) I will use canned tomato wedges for a salad in a pinch. Canned black-eyed and other peas (not English) are satisfactory if a little softer than dried and fresh when cooked. Canned spinach seems a different vegetable than fresh. Those who love it treat it as if it is no relation and pretend it is something else. Many canned vegetables, such as potatoes, need to be rinsed, as their packaging liquid is counterproductive to good tastes. Canned beets are not as good as fresh but can be dressed up satisfactorily if care is taken. Experiment for it can be such a help to have a few canned things on hand.

Dried vegetables and fruit are favorites with me, starting with dried blueberries, cranberries, and cherries, but certainly including dried tomatoes, mushrooms, peas, beans, and lentils. Combined with rice or a grain like quinoa, they can be the basis of an elegant pilaf that would transform a simple roast chicken into a celebration.

SPINACH "BOUILLABAISSE"

This "bouillabaisse" does not contain any fish at all, but a lovely late supper or lunch can be made of this egg dish from Provence. It can easily be doubled if you're very hungry. Sautéed mushrooms (fresh or reconstituted) would be a nice addition, too, if the meal needed to be stretched. It works well with 2 to 4 eggs, depending on how many you are serving.

3 tablespoons olive oil

1 large onion, finely chopped

4 to 5 garlic cloves, peeled and finely chopped

¾ pound potatoes, preferably tiny new ones, scrubbed or peeled and thinly sliced

¼ teaspoon saffron

Dash of hot red pepper sauce

Salt

Freshly ground black pepper

1 10-ounce package frozen chopped spinach, defrosted and squeezed dry

1 bouquet garni (1 parsley stalk, 1 bay leaf, and 1 thyme sprig)

1 tablespoon grated lemon peel (no white attached)

1 egg per person

¼ cup grated imported Parmesan cheese

GARNISH

1 triangle of bread fried in butter per person or 2 toasted pumpernickel rounds per person

Heat the olive oil in a skillet over medium heat. Add the onion and garlic and cook until soft, about 4 minutes. Add the potatoes and let them cook a minute on each side without browning. Transfer to an ovenproof casserole. Add 2 cups boiling water, the saffron, hot pepper sauce, and salt and pepper to taste. Stir the spinach into the casserole, being careful not to break the potato slices. Add the bouquet garni and lemon peel. Cover and allow to simmer until the potatoes are cooked, about 40 minutes. When ready to serve, break 1 egg per person into the pan, sprinkle with the Parmesan, and cook gently over low heat or in a 350° F. oven until the egg whites are set, about 3 minutes on a burner or 5 minutes in the oven. Serve in flat bowls, with an egg in each serving, and garnish with the toast points.

Serves 2 to 4

HOT CARROTS WITH PINE NUTS

This dish is fantastic any time of the year, but I particularly like it in the winter when I need a bright color on the plate. The dressing is a variation on a Caesar salad dressing minus the egg, substituting chicken stock for the oil. Balsamic vinegar, which gives an even subtler flavor, may be used instead of red wine vinegar. If you want to omit the oil, use a nonstick skillet to sweat the carrots and garlic.

2 tablespoons olive oil (optional)
6 carrots, peeled and sliced
2 garlic cloves, peeled and chopped
¼ cup pine nuts
1½ tablespoons capers, drained
2 anchovy fillets, crushed
3 tablespoons red wine vinegar
½ tablespoon Dijon mustard

1 tablespoon chopped oregano, preferably
   fresh
¼ cup fresh or canned chicken stock or
   broth
½ teaspoon Tabasco sauce
Salt
Freshly ground black pepper
½ cup grated imported Parmesan cheese

Heat the olive oil in a large skillet. Add the carrots, garlic, pine nuts, capers, and anchovies and cook over medium heat until the pine nuts begin to brown slightly, about 5 minutes. In a measuring cup, whisk together the vinegar, mustard, oregano, chicken stock, and Tabasco. Season to taste with salt and pepper. Pour over the hot carrots. Serve warm or at room temperature. Garnish with the Parmesan cheese.

Serves 6

HONEY–GINGERED CARROTS

Carrots have a natural sweetness that is enhanced when cooked with honey. The vinegar gives balance and a subtle fruitiness. Several types of honey are available today (orange blossom, clover, wildflower). Experiment with different types until you find one that suits your taste best.

6 carrots, peeled and cut into ½-inch slices
1 tablespoon butter
1 tablespoon chopped fresh ginger
Grated peel (no white attached) of 1
   orange
⅓ cup honey

2 tablespoons raspberry, balsamic, or red
   wine vinegar
2 tablespoons chopped fresh lemon balm
   or mint
Salt
Freshly ground black pepper

Place the carrots in a saucepan with 2 cups of water. Bring to the boil, then reduce the heat and simmer for about 5 minutes. Drain. In the same saucepan, melt the butter over medium-low heat. Add the ginger, orange peel, honey, vinegar, and carrots. Toss until heated through, about 1 minute. Remove from the heat. Add the lemon balm or mint and salt and pepper to taste. Serve hot.

Serves 6 to 8

COMPANY CABBAGE

Perhaps I cook so much cabbage because it keeps in the refrigerator for a week or more and it's always there when I need it. But it's also because I love this recipe—it's so simple and the result is marvelous. Fresh thyme, if you have it, makes all the difference in the world.

1 tablespoon olive oil
1 onion, sliced
2 cups fresh or canned chicken stock or
   broth
1 cabbage, cored and cut into 8 wedges

1 tablespoon thyme leaves
3 tablespoons butter (optional)
Salt
Freshly ground black pepper

In a large skillet, heat the olive oil over medium heat. Add the onion and cook until golden, about 10 to 12 minutes. In a large pot, heat the chicken stock to the boil. Add the sautéed onion, cabbage, thyme leaves, butter if using and salt and pepper to taste. Reduce the heat and simmer, covered, until the cabbage is tender, 15 to 20 minutes.

Serves 6 to 8

SPICY BRUSSELS SPROUTS

Fresh Brussels sprouts, which like their relative, cabbage, keep extremely well, are ideal for this recipe. Frozen Brussels sprouts work, however, and have already been blanched, which makes this a quick side dish. Defrost and treat them as cooked. The sprouts can be covered tightly and refrigerated for up to 1 day. Reheat before serving.

1 tablespoon vegetable oil
¼ cup slivered almonds
½ teaspoon yellow mustard seeds, crushed
¼ teaspoon cumin seeds
¼ teaspoon fennel seeds

3 cups cooked Brussels sprouts, halved
⅛ teaspoon cayenne pepper
1 tablespoon finely chopped fresh ginger
About 1 tablespoon fresh lime juice
½ teaspoon salt

In a large, heavy, nonreactive skillet, heat the oil over moderately high heat for about 30 seconds. Add the almonds and the mustard, cumin, and fennel seeds. Cook, stirring, until the nuts and spices are fragrant and dark, about 15 seconds.

Reduce the heat to moderate and add the Brussels sprouts, cayenne, and ginger. Cook and stir until the vegetables are heated through and the spices are well distributed, about 4 minutes. Add a few tablespoons of water if the vegetables look dry. Season to taste with up to 1 tablespoon of lime juice and the salt and serve hot.

Serves 6

BRAISED CELERY

I often buy a head of celery and use just a stalk or two in a stock. Then when guests drop in on the spur of the moment, and my vegetable bin is empty save for that nearly whole head of celery, I make this very special emergency dish. Defrosted green peas may be added at the end of the cooking time as a variation.

2 small heads of celery
1 small onion, thinly sliced
1 carrot, thinly sliced (optional)
½ cup fresh or canned chicken stock or
   broth

Salt
Freshly ground black pepper
2 teaspoons all-purpose flour
2 teaspoons butter, softened
¼ cup chopped fresh parsley (optional)

Preheat the oven to 325°F. Grease a 10-inch ovenproof dish.

Bring a large pot of water to the boil. Remove the leaves and tough ends from the celery, cut each head in half lengthwise, and add to the boiling water. Return to the boil and cook 8 to 10 minutes. Drain carefully. Place the onion, carrot if using, and chicken stock in the prepared baking dish. Top with the celery. Season to taste with salt and pepper. Cover and bake until tender, 20 to 30 minutes.

In a small bowl, mix the flour and butter together to a smooth paste. Remove the dish from the oven and transfer the vegetables to a platter, leaving the juices in the pan. Whisk the flour and butter mixture into the remaining liquid. Over high heat, quickly bring back to the boil and simmer until thickened, 2 to 3 minutes. Pour over the vegetables and sprinkle with the parsley if desired.

Serves 4

SAUTÉED MUSHROOMS

Mushrooms are lovely by themselves as a side dish or tossed with a green vegetable or pasta. Reserve any tough stems for soup stocks. Dried and reconstituted or canned mushrooms can be substituted for fresh ones.

1 pound mushrooms, cleaned
2 tablespoons butter
Salt

Freshly ground black pepper
1 tablespoon thyme (optional)

Remove any brown or tough stems and slice the mushrooms if large or leave whole if small. Heat the butter in a frying pan. Add the mushrooms and sauté 3 to 5 minutes. Add salt, pepper, and thyme if using to taste.

Serves 4

MUSHROOMS À LA GRECQUE

In the great ice storm of '94, the mushrooms lasted the longest of any vegetable in my friend Laura Bradley's Mississippi home—over ten days.

¼ cup vegetable oil, preferably olive
2 carrots, roughly chopped
1 onion, roughly chopped
1 to 2 garlic cloves, peeled and chopped
½ cup dry white wine
Salt
Freshly ground black pepper

1 pound button mushrooms, cleaned
½ pound tomatoes, peeled, seeded, and
*   roughly chopped, fresh or canned*
2 tablespoons chopped fresh parsley
Bouquet garni of 2 parsley stalks, 2
*   thyme sprigs, and 2 bay leaves*

Heat 2 tablespoons of the oil in a frying pan. Add the carrots, onion, and garlic and sauté until soft. Add the wine and season to taste with salt and pepper. Remove the tough stems of the mushrooms (reserve for stock or soup). Add the whole mushrooms to the vegetables. Add the tomatoes and bouquet garni. Cook 15 to 20 minutes over medium heat. Remove the bouquet garni. Stir in the parsley. Serve hot or cold.

Serves 4 to 6

BROCCOLI SPEARS DRENCHED WITH GARLIC

You really have to like garlic in this dish adapted from one by Julie Sahni—but it's very pretty. It's unusual in that the broccoli is not pre-cooked, and that it is cut into long spears rather than the usual florets.

1 head of broccoli
1½ tablespoons vegetable oil or butter
8 to 10 garlic cloves, peeled

¼ teaspoon turmeric
Salt

Peel the broccoli and cut the broccoli into spears, leaving the long stems attached to the florets. Rinse and drain the spears well. Pat dry.

Heat the oil over medium-high heat in a large skillet. When the oil is hot, add the garlic and cook quickly, stirring, until it turns golden, 1 to 2 minutes. Add the turmeric and the broccoli. Spread the broccoli so that it lies in one layer. Cook 1 minute. Turn the broccoli carefully and cook quickly for another minute.

Reduce the heat, cover the pan, and cook the broccoli until still crisp and dark green, 8 to 10 minutes. Uncover and continue cooking until the moisture evaporates and the broccoli spears are coated with the garlic, 3 to 5 minutes. Season to taste with salt and serve immediately.

Serves 4 to 6

PEPPER MÉLANGE

I always feel a dish with red bell peppers whether fresh or roasted and from the freezer, a can, or a jar, adds interest and freshness to a meal. If you are using a substitute for fresh peppers, add them to the onions after they are charred.

8 red and/or green bell peppers or
    pimientos, halved and seeded
3 onions, quartered or in eighths
1 head of garlic, papery outer husk
    removed
¼ cup olive oil
¼ cup red wine vinegar

2 tablespoons rosemary and thyme,
    mixed, or 2 teaspoons dried
¾ cup grated imported Parmesan cheese
    (optional)
Salt
Freshly ground black pepper

Preheat the oven to 400°F.

Spread the peppers out on 2 greased baking sheets, cut side down. Arrange the onions on top. Brush the vegetables with oil. Wrap the garlic in foil and add to the sheet. Bake, uncovered, for 1 hour. Unwrap the foil from the garlic, remove the garlic cloves from their skins, then stir the peppers, onions, and garlic together. Continue roasting an hour or so, stirring every 30 minutes, until nicely charred.

In a very large bowl, combine the roasted vegetables, garlic, vinegar, herbs, and Parmesan. Season to taste with salt and pepper.

Serves 8 to 10

GINGERED BEETS WITH YOGURT DRESSING

When the vegetable bin yields nothing fresh, this is one of the best side dishes—or salads—I can think of. If you make it ahead, it will still taste good but the beets will "bleed" and tint the sauce. You could also use a vinaigrette dressing if you're out of yogurt.

3 tablespoons butter or oil
1 small to medium onion, chopped
2 tablespoons finely chopped fresh ginger
3 garlic cloves, peeled and finely
   chopped
2 cans whole or sliced beets, drained and
   cut into strips
1 teaspoon salt

Freshly ground black pepper
1 tablespoon chopped fresh mint
   (optional)

DRESSING
1 cup plain yogurt
Juice of 1 lemon
2 tablespoons sugar (optional)

Melt the butter in a skillet over medium heat. Add the onion and ginger and cook until the onions are soft, 3 to 4 minutes, then add the garlic and cook 2 minutes more. Add the beets and toss until mixed well with the onion mixture. Season with salt, pepper, and mint if using. Set aside in a large bowl to cool. Refrigerate.

In a small bowl, combine the yogurt and lemon juice. Just before serving, pour the dressing over the beets and toss gently. Taste for seasoning and add sugar if desired.

Serves 4 to 6

POTATO FLOWERS

These individual gallettes are reminiscent of potatoes Anna, but with far less fat. A food processor or mandoline speeds slicing. Zucchini slices can be prepared in the same manner and baked about 15 minutes.

FOUR GOOD THINGS TO DO WITH CANNED VEGETABLES
Drain and rinse the vegetables, then:
- Serve cold as a salad with a vinegar or lemon and oil vinaigrette. Add canned, drained tomato wedges. Optional additions include fresh or dried herbs, chopped ginger, canned or reconstituted dried mushrooms, canned tuna fish, crab, salmon, or slices of dried ham. (The same thing is also good when served hot.)
- Melt several tablespoons of Beurre Blanc Sauce (page 103) in a saucepan. When hot, add the drained vegetables and stir until heated through. Or melt [butter] in a saucepan, add [chopped shallot or onions,] and cook until soft. Add [lemon juice or red wine vinegar] (or any of the substitutions for Beurre Blanc Sauce), whip in some butter over heat, then add the vegetables. Optional additions include chopped fresh, dried, or packed-in-oil herbs, canned tomato salsa, Mushroom Duxelles (page 101).

2 large all-purpose potatoes, cut into ⅛-inch slices

1 tablespoon olive or peanut oil

Salt

Freshly ground black pepper

- Combine with a diluted can of mushroom soup, chicken and broccoli soup, or cheese soup.
- Melt some butter in a saucepan. Heat until it turns brown. Add the drained vegetables and heat through.

Preheat the oven to 400°F. Spray a baking sheet with nonstick cooking spray. Arrange 5 slices of potato in an overlapping flower design about 4 inches across. Top with 3 smaller slices. Continue making flowers until all the potato slices have been used. Brush each potato flower with some of the oil and lightly salt and pepper them to taste. Place the baking sheet in the hot oven and bake until golden, 25 to 30 minutes.

Serves 6

CAULIFLOWER NIÇOISE

This has a convincingly fresh flavor, although the main ingredient comes from the freezer. Frozen, defrosted broccoli and Brussels sprouts are very nice in this dish as well. A couple of anchovies would enhance the Mediterranean ambience.

1 head of cauliflower or 1 10-ounce box frozen cauliflower

1 tablespoon olive oil

2 tablespoons butter

1 large onion, finely chopped

2 garlic cloves, peeled and finely chopped

1 14½-ounce can chopped Italian plum tomatoes and their juice

2 tablespoons finely chopped fresh parsley

Salt

Freshly ground black pepper

Sugar

Break the cauliflower into florets. Heat the olive oil and butter in a frying pan. Add the onion and garlic and cook until soft. Add the tomatoes, some of their juice, and the parsley. Season to taste with salt, pepper, and sugar. Add the cauliflower and simmer for a further 10 minutes, or until tender. Add more juice if desired.

Serves 4

CRISPY BROWN POTATOES

These potatoes are similar to the pommes frites my son-in-law, Pierre-Henri, craves with his steak. The onion and herbs give the dish additional character. Be sure to use a heavy skillet, one that will retain the heat. The secret is to toss the potatoes occasionally until crispy brown. If you can shake the pan by its handle and cause them all to flip in the air, that's even better than stirring.

¼ cup olive oil

8 medium potatoes, peeled and cut into
  ¾-inch cubes

1 onion, sliced

1 to 2 tablespoons chopped fresh herbs
  (rosemary, thyme, oregano, parsley)

Salt

Freshly ground black pepper

In a large skillet, heat the oil until very hot. Add the potatoes and onion, reduce the heat slightly, and cook for 30 to 40 minutes until they begin to brown, tossing occasionally. Add the herbs and salt and pepper to taste and cook until the potatoes are crispy, yet soft on the inside, 5 to 10 minutes longer.

Serves 8 to 10

MASHED POTATOES

I prefer really soft, lump-free mashed potatoes. If you prefer them this way too, the potatoes really need to be cooked thoroughly. Lumpy mashed potatoes are preferred by those whose ancestors served lumpy ones, so if that is your mission, cook them less. Cream makes for rich potatoes, but to save fat grams, use the hot cooking water from the potatoes or evaporated skim milk. If not serving immediately, pour a little hot liquid over the surface or put plastic wrap directly on the surface and let stand. Alternately, refrigerate up to 2 days in advance, tightly covered or in plastic bags, and reheat, preferably in the microwave.

8 to 10 medium potatoes	1 cup (2 sticks) butter
2 to 3 heads of garlic, peeled	Salt
2 onions, chopped	Freshly ground black pepper
¾ cup heavy cream or milk	

Peel the potatoes and cut into large pieces. Place the potatoes, garlic, and onions in a large saucepan and cover with water. Bring to the boil, reduce the heat, and cook until very tender, about 1 to 1½ hours. Drain in a colander and return to the hot pan. In another saucepan, heat the cream and butter until the butter melts. Place the potatoes over low heat and add half of the hot liquid. Mash or beat until light and fluffy, adding more hot liquid as needed. Season to taste with salt and pepper.

Serves 10 to 12

OVEN-FRIED SWEET POTATO CHIPS

These are so delicious you may want to keep them around as a snack as well as serving them with pork, venison, or roast chicken. A food processor really speeds up the slicing.

3 to 4 medium sweet potatoes, peeled and cut into ¹⁄₁₆-inch-thick slices	¼ teaspoon salt
	2 teaspoons sugar
2 tablespoons vegetable oil or cooking spray	1 teaspoon cinnamon
	¼ teaspoon cayenne pepper

Preheat the oven to 425°F. Lightly spray several baking pans with nonstick cooking spray.

Spread out the potato slices on the baking sheets in a single layer. Brush with the oil or lightly spray with cooking spray.

In a small bowl, mix together the salt, sugar, cinnamon, and cayenne. Sprinkle on the potatoes. Bake until the potatoes are golden brown, 20 to 30 minutes.

Serves 4

DRIED CRANBERRY PILAF

Very "uptown" and trendy, this is an impressive side dish. Dried cranberries can be ordered from mail-order stores or they can be purchased in health food stores or farmers' markets for much less. I stock up on them when I see them. You could substitute raisins or currants. Basmati rice is now available in specialty food stores or the international section of large grocery stores. The pilaf freezes for up to 3 months.

¼ cup (½ stick) butter
1 large onion, chopped
2 cups basmati rice
½ cup dried cranberries

4 cups fresh or canned chicken stock or broth
Salt
Freshly ground black pepper
¼ cup finely chopped fresh parsley

Melt the butter in a large saucepan over medium heat. Add the onion and cook until soft, 5 minutes or so. Add the rice and stir until translucent, 2 to 3 minutes. Add the cranberries and stock and stir well. Bring to the boil, reduce the heat, and simmer until tender, about 18 minutes. Season to taste with salt and pepper. Fluff the rice with a fork. Stir in the parsley just before serving.

Serves 6 to 8

SOUTHERN BROWNED RICE

This recipe from the Duchess of Windsor's cookbook is totally unusual. She claimed it was southern although I've never seen rice made this way in the South. No matter, I love it!

1½ cups long-grain white rice
1½ tablespoons butter

1½ teaspoons salt
3½ cups water

Preheat the oven to 300°F.

Place the rice and butter in an ovenproof skillet and set over medium heat. Cook, stirring, until the rice is golden brown but not burned. Add the salt and water, cover, and put the skillet in the oven. Bake until the rice is done, about 30 minutes.

Serves 4

NOTE: *Brown rice may be used, but increase the cooking time to 45 minutes.*

BERT'S FORTY-CARAT QUINOA

The late Bert Greene was a dear friend. This unusual dish was named after the gold carrots from his cookbook *Greene on Grains*. I couldn't leave his recipe alone, however, and added curry to make it even more golden. Quinoa is a fine-textured grain that was once the staple food of the Incas. It provides a complete protein.

2 tablespoons butter
1 small onion, chopped
¼ teaspoon curry powder
2 small carrots, peeled and chopped
  (about ½ cup)
1⅔ cups fresh or canned chicken stock or
  broth

⅔ cup quinoa, rinsed and drained
¼ teaspoon ground cumin
Salt
Freshly ground black pepper

GARNISH
Chopped fresh parsley

Melt the butter in a medium saucepan over medium-low heat. Add the onion, curry powder, and carrots and cook for 5 minutes. Stir in ⅔ cup of the chicken stock, and bring to the boil. Reduce the heat to medium-low and cook, covered, 20 minutes. Remove the vegetables from the pan with a slotted spoon and puree in a food processor or blender. Return to the pan, add the remaining 1 cup stock, and bring to the boil. Stir in the quinoa and reduce the heat; simmer, covered, over medium-low heat until the quinoa is tender, 12 to 15 minutes. Stir in the cumin and season to taste with salt and pepper. Sprinkle with parsley before serving.

Serves 4

tomatoes, herbs, and crumbled bacon; butter, whipping cream, and Parmesan; sun-dried tomatoes, garlic, oil; shrimp, ginger, garlic, and butter or oil.

Pizza: mundane tomatoes and cheese; pepperoni; mushrooms, fresh vegetables; duck; salmon; dried tomatoes; canned or smoked salmon; oil or butter; cream, herbs, gravlax.

Saltines: peanut butter; sardines; kippers; cheddar cheese; dried salami, other meats.

Scrambled eggs, omelettes: tomato, garlic, oil or butter; grated Swiss, Parmesan, cheddar, blue, saga blue, brie, Camembert; sautéed mushrooms (dried or fresh); ham or dried meat.

Bread, pita, English muffins: grilled or toasted with cheese; topped with any of the above.

OVEN-BAKED ONION RICE

Rice is endlessly versatile, both for family and for company. To dress this dish up, sauté ¾ cup of sliced almonds in butter and add them with the herbs and spices.

¼ cup (½ stick) butter, olive oil, or a
   combination of both
3 onions, sliced
1½ cups long-grain white rice
2 tablespoons chopped parsley, preferably
   fresh
1 tablespoon ground cumin

1 teaspoon paprika
1 teaspoon chili powder
4 to 5 cups fresh or canned beef stock or
   broth
Salt
Freshly ground black pepper

Preheat the oven to 350°F. Butter a 9 × 13-inch baking pan.

Melt the butter in a large skillet over medium heat. Add the onions and sauté until they are a deep mahogany brown, about 20 minutes. Add the rice and cook about 2 minutes longer, until the rice is slightly puffed. Stir in the parsley, cumin, paprika, and chili powder. Pour the onion-rice mixture into the prepared pan. Pour 4 cups of the beef stock over the rice, cover with foil, and bake for 1 hour, removing the foil during the last 10 minutes of baking. (If the rice begins to dry out, add the remaining cup of stock ¼ cup at a time.) Fluff the rice with a fork and season to taste with salt and pepper.

Serves 6 to 8

RICE WITH DRIED FRUIT

A RICE CHECKLIST
Along with pasta, rice is perhaps the most basic pantry ingredient. It can be dressed up (classic risotto Milanese) or down (plain boiled rice), combined with beans for a filling, economical protein, or used to extend more exotic or precious ingredients. It can go in salads, casseroles, side dishes—even dessert! Don't stop with long-grain white rice; I like the nutty scent of basmati so well I use it for most of the dishes I'd regularly served with regular white rice. Plump, pearly short-grain rices for risotto, such as Arborio, are a nice addition, as are brown rices and some of the novelty rices coming out of Louisiana and Texas, such as basmati, Texmati, and pecan rices.

Sometimes when I get home tired and hungry I can't think of what to cook; my brain just doesn't work when I'm that far gone. I always keep these ingredients on my shelf. I have also used 5½ cups cooked rice that I cooked previously and had frozen. The dish goes particularly well with chicken and curries. Reheat in the microwave.

½ teaspoon salt	2 tablespoons butter
1½ cups long-grain rice	1 small onion, chopped
½ cup warm water	Salt
½ cup chopped dried apricots or peaches	Freshly ground black pepper
½ cup raisins, dried cherries, or dried cranberries	Pinch of cinnamon (optional)

In a large saucepan, bring a large quantity of water to the boil. Add the salt. Add the rice, reduce the heat to medium–high, and cook 12 minutes, stirring occasionally. Drain well. Alternately, follow package directions for cooking rice.

Meanwhile, pour the warm water over the apricots and raisins to plump.

Melt the butter in a large saucepan or skillet over medium heat. Add the onion and cook until softened, 4 or 5 minutes. Add the rice and toss.

Drain the fruit well and add to the rice. Season to taste with salt and pepper and the cinnamon if desired.

Serves 4 to 6

COUSCOUS PILAF

Couscous is tiny pasta made from semolina flour. A traditional dish of the North African countries, it is becoming very popular here not only because of its delicious taste but also because the quick variety can be prepared in minutes. It combines well with many foods, such as those in this vegetarian delight. Since I discovered couscous, I've never been without it.

¼ cup (½ stick) butter

3 carrots, peeled and finely chopped

2 cups fresh or frozen green peas

1 cup fresh mushrooms, sliced, or 6 to 8
    dried shiitake mushrooms, soaked and
    drained

1 onion, chopped

2 garlic cloves, peeled and chopped

2 teaspoons lime juice

2 cups couscous

2 to 3 cups fresh or canned chicken stock
    or broth, boiling

¼ cup chopped fresh parsley (optional)

Salt

Freshly ground black pepper

½ cup sliced almonds, toasted

In a large pan, melt the butter over medium-high heat. Quickly sauté the carrots, peas, mushrooms, onion, and garlic until slightly softened, 3 or 4 minutes. Add the lime juice and the couscous and cook for 2 minutes. Stir in the chicken stock and parsley if using, cover the dish, and leave for 5 minutes. Remove the lid, fluff with a fork, and season to taste with salt and pepper. Sprinkle with the sliced almonds.

Serves 6

CAPERS
For such a tiny little vegetable, capers engender very strong sentiments in many who are not fans of their briny, piquant taste. To soften their flavor somewhat, you can try rinsing off their brine before adding them to a dish or, if you do not have the tiny nonpareil variety of capers, chop large capers finely before using and reduce the amount slightly. There are many varieties available, including a vacuum-packed one that is delicious.

PECAN DRESSING

Recently we made an entire pantry Thanksgiving buying nothing but the turkey. We used bread defrosted "fresh" from the freezer for a delicious dressing. I like to make a gracious quantity as it freezes so well up to 3 months and is a good side dish for chicken, beef, or pork as well as turkey.

4 cups chopped pecans

3 cups fresh bread, torn or cut into pieces

5 tablespoons butter, melted

3 tablespoons chopped sage, preferably fresh

1 hot red pepper, chopped (optional)

1 teaspoon cayenne pepper

3 cups fresh or canned chicken or turkey
   stock or broth

Salt

Freshly ground black pepper

Preheat the oven to 350°F. Grease a 9 × 13-inch baking dish.

Mix the pecans, bread, butter, sage, red pepper, and cayenne together. Stir in the stock. Add salt and pepper to taste. Place the dressing in the prepared pan and bake for 30 minutes.

Serves 10 to 12

ORZO WITH LEMON, CAPERS, AND HERBS

This is a very tasty side dish for a simple broiled chicken, pork, or fish. It has a creamy consistency similar to a risotto but without the addition of any butter or cream. The lemon and capers add a nice tart and tangy character.

6 to 7 cups fresh or canned beef stock or
   broth

2 cups orzo (rice-shaped pasta)

Grated peel (no white attached) of
   2 lemons

1/4 cup lemon juice

1/4 cup capers, rinsed and drained

1/2 to 3/4 cup chopped fresh herbs (basil,
   oregano, parsley, thyme, rosemary)

1/4 cup grated imported Parmesan cheese

Salt

Freshly ground black pepper

In a large saucepan, bring the beef stock to the boil. Add the orzo and continue cooking, stirring often to prevent sticking, about 8 to 10 minutes, or until most of the liquid has been absorbed. Turn off the heat, add the lemon peel, lemon juice, capers, herbs, and cheese. Season to taste with salt and pepper. Stir until completely mixed and the pasta is creamy. Serve at once or keep warm in a 250°F. oven, stirring well before serving.

Serves 4 to 6

POTATO GNOCCHI WITH PESTO

The potatoes for gnocchi can be baked in the oven or microwaved to save time. This recipe makes a light dough, similar to a dumpling but with more flavor thanks to the potatoes. To vary, toss the potato dumplings with a light tomato sauce. If desperate, omit the pesto sauce and season with herbs. The gnocchi can be reheated in the microwave on High for 2 to 3 minutes.

6 large baking potatoes

Salt

2 cups bread flour

3 tablespoons pesto sauce, homemade
  or commercial

¾ cup freshly grated imported

Preheat the oven to 450° F.

Bake the potatoes for 1 hour. While they are still hot, scoop the pulp out of the shells and mash with a fork. Season to taste with salt. Knead in the flour to form a dough that holds together and isn't sticky. Sprinkle flour over a work surface and, with the palms of your hands, roll the dough into long thin ropes, about ½ inch in diameter. Cut the ropes into ¾-inch pieces. Place the gnocchi in a single layer on baking sheets dusted with flour and leave at room temperature several hours to dry.

To cook, bring 6 quarts of salted water to the boil in a large pot. Add the gnocchi and simmer until they float to the top, 3 to 5 minutes. Test one to see that it tastes cooked, firm yet tender with no doughy taste. Using a slotted spoon, transfer the delicate gnocchi to a serving bowl. Toss with the pesto sauce and sprinkle with the Parmesan cheese. Serve at once.

Serves 6

DESPERATION PASTA SALAD

This is another dish that I pull together quickly when "there's nothing to eat." Add frozen or blanched veggies (broccoli, carrots, etc.) to make it more substantial or add more pasta or more tuna or some dried tomatoes—anything goes for a quick weeknight supper.

2 cups small pasta shells	*olives, pitted and chopped or sliced*
1 6-ounce can tuna, drained	*1 tablespoon capers, drained*
1 red bell pepper, finely chopped (optional)	*1 tablespoon olive oil*
3 green onions, green and white parts, sliced	*¼ cup red wine vinegar*
	Salt
¼ cup Kalamata, French, or Italian	*Freshly ground black pepper*

In a large Dutch oven, bring a large quantity of water to the boil. Add the pasta shells and cook according to package directions.

Meanwhile, place the tuna, red bell pepper if using, green onions, olives, capers, olive oil, and vinegar in a medium mixing bowl. When the pasta is done, drain it well and add it to the mixing bowl. Toss to combine. Season to taste with salt and pepper and serve on a bed of shredded lettuce if desired.

Serves 4 for lunch, 2 for dinner

SPICY BLACK-EYED PEA AND JICAMA SALAD

Among the dried and canned legumes on my shelf I always have some black-eyed peas. Jicama adds a delicious crunch with a taste like apples and celery, but if jicama is unavailable, you can substitute 2 tart apples, peeled, cored, and cut into matchstick strips, and 2 celery stalks, cut into ¼-inch diagonal slices, or some canned sliced water chestnuts, drained. I hope your herb garden yields cilantro, but if not, you'll get a satisfactory dish with parsley. You can vary the degree of piquancy by choosing a milder or hotter salsa.

3 cups dried black-eyed peas, soaked
  overnight, cooked until soft, or 2
  16-ounce cans, drained
1 8- to 10-ounce jicama, peeled and cut
  into matchstick strips
1 red onion, chopped
4 green onions, white and green parts,
  chopped
1 roasted red bell pepper (page 106), cut
  into strips

¼ cup chopped fresh cilantro or parsley
1 16-ounce jar medium-hot salsa
2 4-ounce cans whole green chiles,
  roughly chopped
2 tablespoons lime juice, preferably fresh
2 teaspoons chili powder
1 teaspoon ground cumin
½ teaspoon cayenne pepper (optional)
Salt
Freshly ground black pepper

In a large bowl, combine the black-eyed peas, jicama, red onion, green onions, red bell pepper, cilantro, salsa, green chiles, lime juice, chili powder, cumin, cayenne if using, and salt and pepper to taste. Toss to combine. Chill at least 4 hours for the flavors to marry. Serve chilled as a salad or at room temperature as a bed for grilled pork or chicken.

Serves 8

JICAMA
A relatively recent arrival to many root cellars, this crunchy, mild-flavored vegetable that looks like a giant potato can be eaten cooked or raw and is like a sweet water chestnut. Because they tend to be very large, keep in the refrigerator, wrapped well, once cut. You may have leftovers if you buy a jicama for a specific recipe, so try using it in place of water chestnuts, radishes, celery, or fennel in salads and salsas, and add it when you'd use potatoes or turnips in stews or soups.

WARM SALAD OF BROCCOLI WITH RED PEPPER, OLIVES, AND FETA

FREEZING FETA
Although feta keeps for a fairly long time in the refrigerator in its own brine, for true long-term storage, the freezer is best. Be sure to pour off the brine before you freeze it. Crumble leftovers on salads or serve heated on toast.

This is a fairly elegant salad; I've even used it as a starter for company. Broccoli is a staple in my refrigerator, there for when I need a green vegetable. Frozen broccoli will work in this recipe, although it's not quite as wonderful. I like to jazz it up with feta in brine, which I keep in the freezer, but crumbled goat cheese or mozzarella cubes would be nice too. Pimientos, a variety of red bell peppers, are handy when no roasted bell peppers are to be found—or when their price goes through the roof!

1 large head of broccoli

2 tablespoons olive oil

4 garlic cloves, peeled and chopped

10 Kalamata olives, pits removed and chopped into large pieces

1 roasted red bell pepper (page 106) or 1 small jar pimientos, chopped

1 tablespoon finely chopped fresh or dried oregano

1 tablespoon finely chopped fresh or dried parsley

4 ounces feta cheese, crumbled

Salt

Freshly ground black pepper

2 to 4 tablespoons lemon juice or red wine, balsamic, or sherry vinegar

Cut the broccoli into bite-size florets. Bring a large pot of salted water to the boil. Add the broccoli, bring back to the boil, and boil for 2 minutes. Drain and rinse the broccoli with cold water to set the color. The broccoli can be refrigerated at this point for several hours. Set aside.

Heat the oil in a large pan. Add the garlic, olives, pepper or pimientos, oregano, and parsley and cook until heated through. When ready to serve, add the broccoli to the pan, crumble the feta cheese over the broccoli, and heat through. Season to taste with salt and pepper. Sprinkle with lemon juice or vinegar to taste and serve warm.

Serves 6 to 8

NEW POTATO AND
RED ONION SALAD

In this substantial salad the bright lemon flavor and the subtle taste of fresh herbs mingle beautifully with the more neutrally flavored new potatoes and artichoke hearts. The salad is even better the next day. For the best taste possible, use tiny red new potatoes and do not overcook them. If you only have larger red potatoes, cut them into quarters after cooking. Canned potatoes can be substituted. They are adequate but not wonderful. Drain, rinse, and add to the artichoke hearts. If oil-packed artichokes are used, use their oil in the vinaigrette and do not rinse them. This salad keeps 3 to 4 days in the refrigerator. It does not freeze.

2 pounds new red potatoes, scrubbed
2 10-ounce boxes frozen artichoke
    hearts, defrosted, or 2 14-ounce cans,
    drained and rinsed
2 medium red onions, thinly sliced

Lemon Vinaigrette (page 65)
Salt
Freshly ground black pepper
½ cup shaved imported Parmesan
    cheese

Place the potatoes in a large pot of salted water, bring to the boil, and cook until tender, 15 to 20 minutes. Drain the potatoes and quarter if large. In a large bowl, toss the potatoes with the artichoke hearts, red onions, and vinaigrette. Season to taste with salt and pepper. Sprinkle with the shaved Parmesan before serving.

Serves 6 to 8

RIBBON SLAW

Cabbage is the ultimate pantry vegetable, as a head will keep in the crisper drawers for as long as six weeks. It can be used in so many different ways, like this colorful slaw. There is extra vinegar in this salad, making it safe to tote, but for safety's sake I'd use store-bought mayonnaise if it's going to sit out for long. This salad is just as good, if not better, the next day.

1 medium head of red cabbage, cored and thinly sliced

1 medium head of green cabbage, cored and thinly sliced

1 to 2 large carrots, peeled and grated

1 green bell pepper, seeded and cut in thin strips (optional)

DRESSING

1 cup mayonnaise

1 tablespoon sugar

¼ cup apple cider vinegar

1 tablespoon milk

1 teaspoon salt

¼ teaspoon dry mustard

½ teaspoon celery seeds

In a large mixing bowl, combine the cabbages, carrots, and green bell pepper if using, mixing well. In a smaller bowl, whisk together the mayonnaise, sugar, vinegar, milk, salt, dry mustard, and celery seeds until smooth. Pour the dressing over the vegetables and toss well to coat. Refrigerate until well chilled or up to 4 days.

Serves 6 to 8

Variation:
Add sliced red onion and chunks of tart apple.

PEAR AND PROSCIUTTO SALAD

Belying its sophisticated appearance, this refreshing recipe is very simple to make. Paper-thin prosciutto is very expensive, but well worth it, as this ham goes very well with fruit.

4 to 6 lettuce leaves
2 pears
2 thin slices prosciutto or country ham

VINAIGRETTE
2 teaspoons Dijon mustard
¼ cup red wine vinegar
½ cup olive oil
Salt
Freshly ground black pepper

Wash the lettuce leaves and pat dry. Stack on top of each other, roll them together, and cut them crosswise into ½–inch strips. Divide the lettuce strips among 4 salad plates. Peel, core, and cut the pears into lengthwise wedges. Arrange them on top of the lettuce shreds. Cut the prosciutto into julienne strips about ⅛ inch wide. Sprinkle over the sliced pears. In a small bowl, whisk together the mustard, vinegar, oil, and salt and pepper to taste. Drizzle the salad with the vinaigrette and serve immediately.

Serves 4

Boston, Bibb, and red leaf lettuce, turnip greens, and spinach should be well washed, thoroughly dried, tightly wrapped in paper toweling, and kept in a plastic bag (air completely expelled) in the refrigerator. I've made it last a couple of weeks this way. Though it seems indestructible, I rarely use iceberg lettuce and can give it no testimonials.

8 BREADS

Cinnamon-Swirled Raisin Nut Loaf ■ Yeast Waffles ■ Crepe Batter ■ Currant Walnut Bread ■ Fruit, Seed, and Nut Bread ■ Braided Basil Ring ■ Focaccia with Fruit and Pecans ■ Onion Quick Bread ■ Chili Corn Muffins ■ Corn Bread Loaf ■ Garlic-Wild Rice Bread ■ Lemon Pepper French Bread ■ Grandmother Kreiser's Powder Puff Dinner Rolls ■ Pumpkin Chocolate Bread ■ Rosemary and Currant Bread Sticks ■ Oat Pecan Bread ■ Trail Mix Tin Can Bread

WHEN ALL IS SAID and done, bread (and all those related foods such as tortillas, rolls, or crepes) is what makes the difference in the pantry. If there is no bread and no wrappers, meals don't stretch as far. There is frequently not even the same feeling of satisfaction even if the rest of the meal is bountiful. I love these breads—my deep brown breads, full of nuts and goodies, my light French bread, and more.

I come from a family of bakers and grocers on my mother's side. It seems we always loved being around food and having what we needed to eat. My grandmother made enough bread each week to feed her family of five plus at least one hired hand out on her Minnesota farm. Perhaps because of that, my mother always stressed that if you had bread, you could get by.

I agree. I love making yeast bread so much that I have not conquered the bread machine. It takes next to no time to make bread dough in a food processor or mixer and I also like kneading it myself. Most yeast breads are flexible. They can be left to rise a long time in the refrigerator or speeded up by rising in the microwave. All one really needs for making bread is yeast, sugar, flour, and water. Everything else is window dressing—nuts, herbs, milk, buttermilk, seasonings, seeds—all are expendable. In fact, if you don't have enough flour to make what you need, take a chance and use some ground breakfast cereal to stretch it.

If yeast is not available, there are always quick breads. They require baking powder and salt or baking soda, in addition to flour, cornmeal, or another grain. Even eggs are optional if you don't have any!

Crepe batter is another easy substitute—it only requires flour and a liquid, but it is much better with the addition of an egg. Made ahead, frozen, and defrosted, crepes make life very easy. Fill them with any leftovers, plus a bit of sauce, or even jams and jellies. You will impress the stonyhearted. If you are desperate for a bread or wrapper, make them at the last minute.

Breads are not just necessary for the stomach, they are good for the senses. Nothing makes you feel abundantly provided for like the smell of baking bread.

CINNAMON-SWIRLED RAISIN NUT LOAF

This bread perfumes the entire house with the homey aromas of cinnamon and freshly baked bread. I prefer the bread toasted with a nice cup of hot tea. Plumped raisins always seem to work better than nonplumped ones in a yeast bread. If you want a darker bread heat ¼ cup of the liquid from the raisins in place of the plain water. This bread freezes for 2 to 3 months.

2 packages active dry yeast

1 tablespoon granulated sugar

¼ cup warm water (105°F. to 115°F.)

¼ cup (½ stick) butter or margarine, softened

¼ cup molasses

½ cup milk

2 eggs

3 to 4 cups bread flour

½ teaspoon salt

1 tablespoon ground cinnamon

1 cup raisins, plumped in hot water, preferably overnight, drained

1 cup chopped pecans

SWIRL

4 tablespoons (½ stick) butter, softened

2 tablespoons granulated sugar

1 tablespoon cinnamon

GLAZE

½ cup confectioners' sugar

3 to 4 teaspoons warm water

1 teaspoon vanilla extract

STORING FLOUR

I keep my flour, still in its original bag, in a clear, airtight container. That way I can see what kind it is without having to guess or make labels. If you prefer to get rid of the bag, tear off the identifying label and either tape it to the outside of the canister or slip it inside, between the flour and the outside, so it can be seen. White flour will generally keep 3 to 6 months on the shelf or up to a year in the refrigerator or freezer. Whole wheat flour contains more oil than does white, and may deteriorate more quickly.

Preheat the oven to 350° F. Grease two 9 × 5 × 3-inch loaf pans.

Dissolve the yeast and sugar in the warm water. In a food processor, mix together the butter, molasses, milk, and eggs. Add the yeast mixture. To this mixture, add 2 cups of the flour, the salt, and cinnamon. Stir in more flour as needed to make a smooth dough. Knead until the dough is elastic and soft as a baby's bottom, about 1 minute. Place in an oiled plastic bag or bowl. Seal or cover with plastic wrap. Set in a warm place and let double, about 1 hour. By hand, knead in the raisins and the nuts until very well distributed. Roll the dough into a 3 × 12-inch rectangle. Spread the dough with the softened butter, and then sprinkle with the sugar and cinnamon. Roll up very tightly lengthwise, cut in half to form 2 loaves, pinch the ends under, and place in the pans. Let rise again until doubled, about 1 hour. Bake on the middle rack of the oven until golden, about 35 to 40 minutes, and the bread sounds hollow when tapped on the bottom. (It should register 200°F. on an instant-reading thermometer.) Remove from the oven and turn out onto a wire rack to cool. Drizzle the glaze over the cooled loaves. To make the glaze, mix together the confectioners' sugar, water, and vanilla until smooth and of a pouring consistency.

Makes 2 loaves

YEAST WAFFLES

It isn't necessary to wait for desperation times to make these yeast waffles, adapted from *Emory Seasons.* They really add a lot of dash to an otherwise frugal meal. Serve with berries or jam, sour cream or yogurt, pancake or maple syrup. Leftover cooked waffles freeze well for a month or two, but if you plan to freeze them, undercook them just slightly.

1 package active dry yeast
¼ cup warm water (105°F. to 115°F.)
1 tablespoon sugar
2 eggs
1 teaspoon salt

½ cup vegetable oil
3 cups all-purpose flour
2 cups milk
Oil or butter

In a mixing bowl, dissolve the yeast in the warm water with the sugar. Mix in the eggs, salt, and oil. Whisk in the flour and milk alternately, beginning and ending with the flour. The batter will be thin. Cover and refrigerate ½ hour or overnight. Stir the batter down. Heat your waffle iron, using oil or butter if desired or necessary. Ladle in about ½ cup batter per waffle. Cook until golden brown, according to your waffle iron directions.

Makes 10 waffles

CREPE BATTER

Crepes are magical wrappers that enhance what might otherwise seem mundane. Like pasta, they may be made from water, omitting the milk and eggs—tenderness and flavor will be sacrificed, but it will work! The crepes may be refrigerated or frozen, tightly wrapped. Defrost them and serve at room temperature or reheat briefly in the oven, filled or unfilled.

1 cup milk
1 cup all-purpose flour
1 egg

1 egg yolk
½ teaspoon salt
2 tablespoons vegetable oil or butter

Whisk together the milk, flour, egg, egg yolk, and salt. Let sit at least ½ hour or up to overnight in the refrigerator. When ready to cook, thin with ½ cup water or milk if necessary; the batter should have the consistency of milk. Heat a small nonstick skillet with a little oil or butter over medium-high heat. Pour a small ladleful of batter into the pan, swirling to cover the bottom. When lightly brown, about 1 minute, turn over; let the other side brown slightly, 30 to 45 seconds. Turn out onto a rack to cool. Repeat with the remaining batter until it is all used.

Makes 25 crepes

CURRANT WALNUT BREAD

I crave this bread, a rich, deep, dark beauty of a loaf, often. There is little room for bread between the nuts and raisins, but each bite is delicious. Rolled in flour, it is a startling contrast of dark and white, like a snowcapped peak, and the combination of grains gives it a nice texture. It freezes up to 3 months.

2 packages active dry yeast

1½ cups warm water (105°F. to 115°F.)

¼ cup molasses

2 teaspoons salt

1 tablespoon cocoa powder

1 tablespoon instant coffee granules

2 tablespoons vegetable oil

¾ cup rye flour

¾ cup cornmeal

2 cups currants, plumped in 1 cup warm water for 30 minutes and drained

2 cups chopped walnuts

2 cups whole wheat flour

1 to 2 cups bread flour

Preheat the oven to 375°F.

In a large mixing bowl, dissolve the yeast in the warm water with the molasses. Stir in the salt, cocoa, coffee, and vegetable oil. Add the rye flour, cornmeal, currants, and walnuts and stir until well combined. Add the whole wheat flour and stir. Gradually add enough of the bread flour to make a firm dough. Turn out onto a floured surface and knead until smooth, about 8 to 10 minutes, adding a little flour as necessary. Place in a greased bowl, cover, and let rise until doubled, about 1 hour. Punch down and shape into a round or long free-form loaf; roll in flour to coat generously. Place on a greased baking sheet and let rise again until doubled, about 45 minutes. Slash across or in a crisscross design in the top.

Bake the bread until it sounds hollow when tapped on the bottom, about 35 to 45 minutes. (The temperature should register 200°F. on an instant-reading thermometer.) Cool on a rack.

Makes 1 loaf

FRUIT, SEED, AND NUT BREAD

I'm constantly searching for new breads. I'd bake bread every day if I could! More and more I like breads with a variety of textures—nuts, seeds, raisins. I made this up one day to use up some odds and ends in my baking pantry and everyone loved it. It's great toasted for breakfast or as a filling snack on a day's hike on the Appalachian Trail. Feel free to vary the ingredients by substituting other dried fruits (finely chopped) for the currants or using different nuts, like walnuts—it's a delicious way to clean out the cupboards! This bread freezes well for 2 to 3 months.

1 package active dry yeast

1 tablespoon molasses

1 cup warm water (105°F. to 115°F.)

2½ to 3 cups bread flour

1 tablespoon cocoa powder

1½ teaspoons ground cinnamon

2 teaspoons salt

¼ cup bran cereal

2 tablespoons currants or raisins

2 tablespoons roughly chopped sunflower seeds

2 tablespoons roughly chopped pine nuts

2 tablespoons roughly chopped pecans, walnuts, hazelnuts, or almonds

GLAZE

1 egg beaten with 1 tablespoon water

EGG GLAZES
Depending on how much yolk and/or water is in your glaze, your loaf will appear glossier or deeper brown. To determine which glaze you prefer, mix a whole egg with a tablespoon of water, an egg yolk with a tablespoon of water or milk, and an egg white with a tablespoon of water. Paint in strips down a "test" loaf of bread, and compare the glazes. Choose one as your "signature" glaze.

Preheat the oven to 350°F.

In a measuring cup, dissolve the yeast and molasses in the warm water. In a mixing bowl, combine 2 cups of the flour, the cocoa, cinnamon, salt, bran cereal, and the yeast mixture. Turn out onto a floured surface and knead, adding more flour as needed, until the dough is elastic and smooth as a baby's bottom. Knead in the currants, sunflower seeds, pine nuts, and pecans. Place in an oiled plastic bag or bowl. Seal or cover with plastic wrap and let double, about 1 hour. Knock down the dough, shape it into a round, and place it on a greased baking sheet. Let double again, about 45 minutes.

Brush the loaf with the egg glaze and bake 1 to 1½ hours, or until a toothpick inserted in the center comes out clean. (The temperature should register 200°F. on an instant-reading thermometer.) Cool on a rack.

Makes 1 loaf

BRAIDED BASIL RING

MILK IN BREADS
Milk adds nutrients to the dough as well as giving a browner crust and a creamier-colored crumb. The resulting bread lasts longer than those made with water. Don't hesitate to substitute reconstituted powdered milk for fresh in any of these bread recipes; it will work just fine.

This is so lovely and such a special dinner companion it will be considered a special treat.

¾ cup warm milk (105°F. to 115°F.)
¼ cup warm water (105°F. to 115°F.)
2 tablespoons sugar
1 package active dry yeast

2¾ to 3¼ cups bread flour
3 teaspoons dried basil
1 teaspoon salt
2 tablespoons butter or margarine

Preheat the oven to 400°F. Grease a baking sheet.

Combine the milk and water in a small bowl. Add 1 tablespoon sugar and the yeast and stir to dissolve. In a mixer or food processor, combine 2 cups flour, 1 tablespoon sugar, 2 teaspoons basil, and the salt. Add the warm liquid and knead or process until a soft dough forms. Add the remaining flour, ½ cup at a time, until the dough is elastic and soft as a baby's bottom—about 1 minute in a food processor, 10 minutes by hand. Place the dough in a lightly oiled bowl or plastic bag and cover with plastic wrap or seal. Set in a warm place to rise until doubled, about 1 hour. When the dough has doubled, punch down, knead a couple of times, and divide into 3 equal pieces. Roll and stretch each piece into a rope approximately 20 to 24 inches long. Braid the ropes and place on the baking sheet. Form the braid into a circle and pinch the ends to seal. Cover with plastic wrap to prevent a skin forming and let sit until doubled, 30 to 45 minutes.

When doubled, place on the middle rack in the oven and cook until done (golden on top and sounds hollow when the bottom is tapped), about 25 minutes. (The temperature should register 200°F. on an instant-reading thermometer.) Melt the butter and brush on the ring. Sprinkle the ring with the remaining teaspoon of basil and transfer to a wire rack to cool.

Makes 1 loaf

FOCACCIA WITH FRUIT AND PECANS

This combination of sweet fruit and pecans and crusty, flavorful exterior is beguiling. I once made the mistake of leaving one on a rack to cool while I was finishing preparing a supper party. My houseguest and my favorite former husband kept wandering in to break off pieces until they'd polished off the whole thing! By using the food processor to knead the dough and the microwave to facilitate the first rising, you can have a freshly baked focaccia in a little over 1 hour. Sound impossible? Well, just wait until you try this. It freezes for 3 months.

5 tablespoons olive oil
½ cup currants or chopped raisins
2½ to 3 cups bread flour
1 teaspoon salt
1 teaspoon sugar
1 package 50% faster or RapidRise yeast

¾ cup hot water (130°F.)
½ cup chopped toasted pecans
2 tablespoons chopped fresh rosemary
½ cup grated imported Parmesan
   cheese

Preheat the oven to 400°F. Lightly grease a baking sheet.

Pour 3 tablespoons of the olive oil into a small microwave-safe glass bowl and heat at full power in the microwave until very hot, 30 to 45 seconds. Stir in the currants and heat an additional 20 seconds, then set them aside to plump.

In a mixer or processor bowl fitted with the steel blade, combine 2½ cups flour, the salt, sugar, and yeast. Mix. Add the hot water. Knead until soft, adding additional flour as needed to eliminate stickiness.

Add the oil and raisins (if using a food processor reserve half), the pecans, and rosemary and knead the dough sufficiently to mix in the fruit, nuts, and herb. (Knead in the rest of the raisins by hand if half was done with a food processor.)

Form the dough into a ball. With your thumbs, punch a hole to form a doughnut shape and place in an oiled plastic bag or the processor bowl. If in a bowl, cover loosely with a damp tea towel or plastic wrap. Place in the microwave. Place an 8–ounce glass of water in the back of the microwave.

Lower the microwave power to 10% or the next to the lowest power set-

KILLING YEAST

It sounds a bit vicious to talk about killing yeast, but it is an easy thing to do if you don't know the rules. The rules are simple. For active dry yeasts, liquids that are in direct contact with the yeasts should be between 105° F. and 115° F. The quick-rising or rapid-rising yeasts are usually mixed with flour and so have less contact with the water and can take a higher water temperature. If perchance the yeast is killed and the bread doesn't rise, all is not lost. Dissolve a new package of yeast and a bit more sugar in a little more liquid. Knead it into the bread and proceed with the recipe. (More flour might be necessary to offset the additional liquid.)

ting. Heat for 3 minutes. Rest for 3 minutes. Repeat heating for 3 minutes and resting for 3 minutes. Heat for the third time 3 minutes but rest 6 minutes until the dough has doubled in bulk.

Remove the dough from the processor bowl, punch down, and knead by hand a few seconds. Roll the dough into a 9 x 13-inch rectangle and place on the prepared baking sheet. Brush with the remaining 2 tablespoons olive oil and sprinkle with the Parmesan. Allow the dough to rise again, about 20 minutes, or until nearly doubled. Bake until the focaccia is puffy and golden brown, about 25 minutes. Cool on a wire rack and cut into squares to serve.

Serves 6 to 8

ONION QUICK BREAD

Cooked onions are one of my favorite seasonings, so I'm always looking for a way to work them into a meal. This bread features cooked onions and can be combined quickly—it's over the top! It freezes up to 3 months.

¼ cup (½ stick) butter
2 medium onions, chopped
3 cups all-purpose flour
1½ tablespoons baking powder
1½ teaspoons salt
2 tablespoons sugar

½ cup fresh or canned beef stock or broth
1 cup fresh or powdered buttermilk,
*   mixed according to package directions*
½ to 1 teaspoon freshly ground black
*   pepper*

Preheat the oven to 350°F. Grease a 9 × 5 × 3-inch loaf pan.

Melt the butter in a skillet, add the onions, and cook over low heat until very soft, about 10 minutes. Stir or sift together the flour, baking powder, salt, and sugar in a medium mixing bowl. Combine the stock and buttermilk and add to the dry ingredients. Add the cooked onions and the pepper and stir until just combined. Pour the mixture into the prepared pan and bake until brown, 50 to 55 minutes. Cover the top of the bread with aluminum foil and continue to cook until cooked through, a skewer comes out clean, and the bottom and top are brown, 20 to 30 minutes longer. (The temperature should register 200°F. on an instant-reading thermometer.) Turn out onto a rack to cool.

Makes 1 loaf

CHILI CORN MUFFINS

These muffins are delightfully moist, thanks to the addition of creamed corn. Don't let the peppers scare you—they are only mildly hot. For a spicier muffin increase the red pepper flakes to suit your taste or throw in a couple more diced jalapeños or chili peppers. If you don't have fresh jalapeños, heat dried peppers in water and drain, or use part of another can of canned chiles. These muffins freeze well for 2 to 3 months. Reheat wrapped in foil in a 350°F. oven for 20 minutes.

1½ cups all-purpose flour
1 cup yellow cornmeal
2 tablespoons sugar
2 teaspoons baking powder
½ teaspoon salt
¼ teaspoon red pepper flakes
2 jalapeño peppers, chopped (optional)

¾ cup fresh or powdered buttermilk,
  mixed according to package directions
¼ cup olive oil
2 eggs
1 4-ounce can green chiles, chopped
1 8-ounce can creamed corn

Preheat the oven to 400°F. Grease a 12-cup muffin pan.

In a large bowl, mix together the flour, cornmeal, sugar, baking powder, salt, red pepper flakes, and jalapeños if using. In another bowl, whisk together the buttermilk, olive oil, and eggs; stir in the green chiles and creamed corn. Pour the liquid mixture into the dry ingredients and mix until just blended. Ladle the batter into the prepared muffin pan. Bake on the middle rack of the oven 20 to 25 minutes, or until golden brown. Remove from the oven and let cool on a wire rack for about 10 minutes.

Makes 12 muffins

CORN BREAD LOAF

This corn bread loaf is a slight variation on traditional skillet corn bread. The addition of corn kernels and fresh thyme adds an interesting flavor and texture to these hearty slices. Combined quickly from ingredients I always have on hand, the hour-plus baking time allows me to get the main course and vegetables organized. The smell of homemade corn bread keeps everyone waiting patiently. It freezes for 2 months.

Cornmeal, for dusting
1½ cups all-purpose flour
1¼ cups yellow cornmeal
1 tablespoon sugar
1 teaspoon baking powder
1 teaspoon baking soda
2 teaspoons salt

3 eggs
⅓ cup peanut oil
1 cup fresh buttermilk, milk, or powdered buttermilk, mixed according to package directions
1 cup fresh or frozen corn kernels
1 tablespoon chopped fresh thyme

Preheat the oven to 350°F. Grease a 9 × 5 × 3-inch loaf pan, dust with cornmeal, and set aside.

In a large bowl, stir together the flour, cornmeal, sugar, baking powder, baking soda, and salt. In another bowl, whisk together the eggs, oil, buttermilk, corn kernels, and thyme. Stir the liquid mixture into the dry ingredients until just combined. Pour the batter into the prepared pan. Bake 15 minutes, reduce the heat to 325°F., and continue baking about 50 to 55 minutes longer, or until a wooden skewer inserted into the center comes out clean. Cool on a wire rack for 20 minutes before slicing.

Serves 6 to 8 (1 loaf)

GARLIC-WILD RICE BREAD

This hearty, dense bread gets a surprisingly good crunchy texture from wild rice. It is perfect with soups, stews, or salads and stands up well to any dish. If you desire a crunchier, nuttier texture, decrease the cooking time of the wild rice to 20 to 25 minutes. It freezes for 2 to 3 months.

1 tablespoon cornmeal
1¼ cups wild rice
Salt
1 package active dry yeast
1 tablespoon sugar
1 cup warm water (105°F. to 115°F.)
2 teaspoons salt
5 tablespoons olive oil
2 tablespoons chopped fresh rosemary

1 tablespoon cumin
1 tablespoon cracked pepper
2 to 3 teaspoons peeled and finely
chopped garlic (about 2 cloves)
2½ to 3½ cups bread flour

G L A Z E
1 egg beaten with 1 tablespoon water

Preheat the oven to 350°F. Grease a baking sheet and sprinkle with the cornmeal.

In a large colander or strainer, rinse the wild rice under cold water for 3 minutes. Drain. Place the rice with enough salted water to cover by 1 inch in a 2-quart saucepan. Bring to the boil, reduce the heat, cover, and simmer for 35 to 40 minutes, until the rice is cracked and has a very slight crunch to it. Drain and coarsely chop in a food processor. Set aside.

Dissolve the yeast with the sugar in the warm water. In a large bowl or food processor, mix together the salt, olive oil, rosemary, cumin, pepper, garlic, and 2½ cups of the flour and stir into the dissolved yeast. Knead until well mixed. Add the chopped wild rice and enough of the remaining flour to make a stiff dough. On a floured board, knead the dough 8 to 10 minutes until smooth and elastic (or knead 1 minute in the food processor). The dough will feel heavy. Place in an oiled plastic bag, seal, and let double in a warm place, about 1 hour or longer. Remove the dough from the bag, divide in half, and shape into 2 rounds. Place on the prepared baking sheet. Let double again, about 45 minutes. Brush the glaze evenly on the loaves. Slash the top of each loaf.

WILD RICE
There are two major kinds of wild rice readily available in the United States. The grains of the "Canadian" or its similar counterpart from Minnesota and the northern Midwest are a bit larger than the other, the Californian; you may need to vary cooking time a few minutes according to the type. The best test is to remove some before the end of the cooking time and taste it. You may also decide to add more water to the northern type.

To store wild rice for any period of time, use the freezer. Wild rice is a grass, not a grain, so it doesn't keep well more than 3 months on the shelf. If you need longer shelf life and less expense, try one of the wild and long-grain rice mixes. The wild rice in this combination package is precooked and processed to reduce its cooking time to match that of the accompanying rice, so as an added advantage it shortens your cooking time.

Bake 55 to 60 minutes, or until the bottoms sound hollow when tapped. (The temperature should register 200°F. on an instant-reading thermometer.) If the bread should begin to brown too much, cover loosely with foil after 30 minutes of baking. Cool on a wire rack.

Makes 2 loaves

LEMON PEPPER FRENCH BREAD

Lemon and pepper add a fresh hot taste to this traditional loaf. This is an excellent choice for a pasta or fish meal and is best eaten the same day it is baked. To refresh it, run quickly under tap water to dampen and re-heat in a 400°F. oven for 5 minutes. It freezes for 3 months.

2½ to 3½ cups bread flour
1 package active dry yeast
2 teaspoons salt
1½ teaspoons sugar
1 cup hot water (115°F.)
2 tablespoons grated lemon peel (no white attached)

1 tablespoon freshly ground black pepper
Cornmeal, for sprinkling

GLAZE
1 egg beaten with 1 tablespoon water

Preheat the oven to 400°F.

In a food processor or mixer, combine 2½ cups of the flour, the yeast, salt, and sugar. Add the hot water, lemon peel, and pepper. Process or knead to make a soft dough, adding more of the remaining flour if needed. (Allow 1 minute for a food processor or 5 to 10 minutes in a mixer.) Place in an oiled plastic bag or bowl and turn to coat. Seal or cover and let rise until doubled, about 1 hour. Punch down. Roll and shape the dough into 2 long loaves. Place on a baking sheet sprinkled with the cornmeal. Let double again, about 45 minutes.

Brush the loaves with the egg glaze. Slash the top of each loaf 2 or 3 times with a sharp knife. Place on the middle rack of the oven with a small cake pan of boiling water on the bottom rack. Bake until the crusts are crisp and the bottoms sound hollow when tapped, 20 to 25 minutes. (The temperature should register 200°F. on an instant-reading thermometer.) Cool on wire racks.

Makes 2 loaves

GRANDMOTHER KREISER'S POWDER PUFF DINNER ROLLS

This is known to generations of my family as "Grandmother Kreiser's" recipe (although she was really my great-aunt). Her husband, my great-uncle Harry (who is 100 years old), loved it when she cooked this recipe because the rolls were so soft and had just a touch of sweetness. She always made the rolls with cake yeast, but I find the recipe works perfectly well with active dry yeast. These are very traditional, old-time rolls—light enough to powder your face one cousin said—and perfect for lunch or dinner. The dough may be kneaded in the food processor if you prefer. The rolls freeze well for 2 to 3 months.

1 package active dry yeast

4 tablespoons sugar

½ cup warm water (105°F. to 115°F.)

¾ cup fresh milk or reconstituted powdered milk, mixed according to package directions

3 tablespoons butter or margarine

2 teaspoons salt

1 egg, lightly beaten

3½ to 4½ cups bread flour

GLAZE

3 tablespoons fresh milk or reconstituted powdered milk, mixed according to package directions

2 tablespoons sugar

Dissolve the yeast and 1 tablespoon of the sugar in the warm water. Scald the milk by heating it almost to the boil; small simmering bubbles will appear around the edge of the pan. Add the remaining 3 tablespoons sugar, the butter, and salt to the milk and let the mixture cool to warm (105°F. to 115°F.). Add the lightly beaten egg and the yeast mixture; then mix in 2 cups bread flour. Beat with a wooden spoon to a smooth dough. Turn out onto a floured board and knead, adding flour as needed, until elastic and smooth as a baby's bottom. Place in an oiled bowl, cover with plastic wrap, and set aside to rise in a warm place until doubled.

Preheat the oven to 350°F. Lightly grease a 9 × 13-inch baking pan. Punch down the dough, and knead it lightly. To shape, pinch off small pieces of dough and roll them into balls. Place them touching each other in the pan, and let double. Bake 15 minutes.

EVER READY BISCUIT MIX
Sift together 10 cups self-rising flour, 3 teaspoons salt, and 4 teaspoons baking powder. Cut in 2 cups cold vegetable shortening. Store in the refrigerator in an airtight container. To use, gently combine 1 part milk or buttermilk with 2 parts mix. Roll or pat out 1 inch thick. Cut 2-inch rounds. Bake at 500°F. for 8 to 10 minutes.

Meanwhile make the glaze by mixing together the milk and sugar. Remove the rolls from the oven, brush with the glaze, and return them to the oven for 5 to 10 more minutes. Remove them from the pan and cool on a rack.

Makes 24

PUMPKIN CHOCOLATE BREAD

Ifirst made this when I had some pumpkin puree left over after Thanksgiving pie making. Now I always make sure to keep a small can on the shelf just for this incredibly moist quick bread. It lasts for days, ready to be sliced at a moment's notice, when friends drop by over the holidays or for a lift after a session of wrapping presents.

½ cup (1 stick) butter or margarine, melted
1 cup firmly packed brown sugar, light or dark
2 eggs, lightly beaten
1 cup canned pumpkin
1¾ cups all-purpose flour
½ teaspoon salt
1 teaspoon baking soda

¼ teaspoon baking powder
1 teaspoon ground cinnamon
¼ teaspoon ground cloves
½ teaspoon ground nutmeg
¼ teaspoon mace
1 cup chocolate chips (6 ounces)
½ cup chopped nuts (pecans, almonds, or walnuts)

Preheat the oven to 350°F. Grease and flour a 9 × 5 × 3-inch loaf pan.

Stir the butter and sugar together in a bowl. Add the eggs, one at a time, beating well after each addition. Mix in the pumpkin.

In a small mixing bowl, sift together the flour, salt, baking soda, baking powder, cinnamon, cloves, nutmeg, and mace. Add to the pumpkin mixture and stir until just combined. Gently stir in the chocolate chips and nuts. Pour into the prepared pan and bake 55 to 65 minutes, or until a wooden skewer inserted in the center comes out clean. Let cool in the pan 10 minutes, then turn onto a wire rack to finish cooling.

Makes 1 loaf

ROSEMARY AND CURRANT BREAD STICKS

These crisp herb and currant bread sticks are chock full of flavor and texture and are great with soups or stews or as an appetizer to munch on with drinks. They have very little fat, but they taste so good! The olive oil, currants, and rosemary are omitted from the initial rising to speed the process. Try this with any favorite dried fruit. They freeze well for 2 to 3 months.

2 packages active dry yeast
2 teaspoons sugar
1/4 cup warm water (105°F. to 115°F.)
3/4 cup milk, at room temperature
1 teaspoon salt
2 1/2 to 3 cups bread flour
1/4 cup olive oil
1 1/2 to 2 tablespoons chopped fresh or
   dried rosemary

1/4 cup currants, plumped in warm water
   for 30 minutes, drained, and patted
   dry

GLAZE
1 egg beaten with 2 teaspoons water
Kosher salt

SLOW-RISE LOAVES
Salt inhibits the action of yeast, causing the dough to rise more slowly. Slow rising adds to the flavor of the bread, as does the salt itself. Salt also strengthens the gluten in the bread.

In the summer I derive an enormous amount of earth-mother satisfaction from putting my covered dough out on the deck to rise in the summer sun. In the winter, I fill a pan with hot water and place the bowl of dough on top. The trick is to keep the dough warm without raising the temperature enough to kill yeast (I use 120° F. as my guideline).

Alternately, if the house is cool, I make the bread dough before going to bed and let it rise overnight. The next morning the bread has risen perfectly and is ready to go in the oven.

Preheat the oven to 375°F.

In a small bowl, dissolve the yeast and sugar in the warm water. When dissolved, combine with the warm milk in a food processor or mixing bowl. Add the salt and 2 cups of the flour and beat until a dough is formed. Add the remaining flour, 1/2 cup at a time, kneading in the food processor or mixer until elastic and smooth as a baby's bottom. Place the dough in an oiled plastic bag or bowl and seal or cover with plastic wrap. Set aside to rise in a warm place until doubled in bulk, about 1 hour.

When doubled, punch down and knead in the olive oil, rosemary, and currants. When the dough is smooth, divide it into 16 pieces and roll each one into a rope 14 to 15 inches long. Place them on a greased baking sheet and cover lightly with plastic wrap. Let rise again until doubled, about 45 minutes.

When doubled, brush with the egg glaze and sprinkle with kosher salt. Bake until lightly browned, about 25 to 30 minutes. Cool on wire racks.

Serves 16

OAT PECAN BREAD

SWEETENERS
Yeast breads are always happiest with some sugar or other sweetener for the yeast to feed on, which increases fermentation. Sugar also adds flavor, tenderizes, and adds color to the crust when it caramelizes. Too much sugar, however, causes the yeast to be sluggish. For a non-sweet dough the usual amount is 1 to 2 tablespoons per three cups of flour.

Sugar and honey are generally my sweeteners of choice. Honey, like maple syrup, is twice as sweet as sugar, so use half as much when it is substituted. Some modification of the amount of liquids in the dough will also be needed if you interchange sugar and liquid sweeteners. Brown sugars can be substituted for white sugar in a one-to-one ratio.

This rough country loaf is very pretty—white oatmeal against a beige round loaf. It is very earthy with a chewy texture. Not too heavy and very healthy, it is very slow rising. I use it in the country, toasted, with peanut butter or goat cheese for a hearty lunch. It freezes up to 3 months.

2 packages active dry yeast
¼ cup honey
¾ cup warm water (105°F. to 115°F.)
3 tablespoons butter or margarine, melted
1 egg, lightly beaten
1½ teaspoons salt

½ cup plus 1 tablespoon old-fashioned rolled oats
½ cup coarsely chopped pecans
1 cup whole wheat flour
1½ to 2 cups bread flour
1 egg white beaten with 1 tablespoon water

Preheat the oven to 375°F. Lightly grease a baking sheet.

Dissolve the yeast with the honey in the warm water in a large bowl. Add the butter, egg, and salt and beat until well mixed. Add the ½ cup of oats and pecans and stir well. Stir in the whole wheat flour, then add the bread flour, ½ cup at a time, to make a stiff dough. Knead in a mixer or turn out onto a floured surface and knead until smooth, about 10 to 15 minutes. The dough will feel sticky due to the honey, but do not increase the flour.

Place in a lightly oiled bowl, cover with plastic wrap, and let rise in a warm place until nearly doubled, about 1½ to 2 hours. When doubled, punch down, divide in half, and shape into 2 rounds. Place each loaf on the prepared baking sheet, cover, and let rise again until doubled, about 45 minutes. Brush the loaves with egg white, sprinkle with the remaining tablespoon of oats, and slash an ✕ across the top of each loaf.

Bake until the loaves sound hollow when tapped on the bottom, 35 to 40 minutes. (The temperature should register 200°F. on an instant-reading thermometer.) Transfer to wire racks to cool.

Makes 2 loaves

TRAIL MIX TIN CAN BREAD

I long wanted a bread to take hiking that would stay moist for a number of days and that could be made a day or two before I left. My friend Bernard Clayton's Hobo Bread from his book, *Bernard Clayton's New Complete Book of Breads,* fit the bill. I decided to expand the recipe, using dried fruit bits sometimes and other times raisins, as a replacement for trail mix and granola. Toast the rounds and eat them with cream cheese, goat cheese, or honey for breakfast or a late afternoon snack—it's a sheer delight. The bread also makes a wonderful gift. It freezes up to 3 months.

2 cups dried fruit bits, dried cranberries,
    cherries, blueberries, currants, or 1 cup
    each light (golden) and dark raisins
2 cups hot water
4 teaspoons baking soda
1½ cups sugar

¼ cup vegetable oil
½ teaspoon salt
3 cups all–purpose flour
1 cup chopped walnuts or pecans
½ teaspoon ground cinnamon (optional)
½ teaspoon almond extract (optional)

Preheat the oven to 350°F. Grease and flour 2 1–pound coffee cans or 2 9 × 5 × 3–inch loaf pans and line the bottom with wax paper. Grease and flour the wax paper.

Place the fruit bits or raisins in a large bowl, cover with the hot water, and stir in the baking soda. Cover with plastic wrap and leave overnight to plump. All of the liquid is used in the batter, so don't drain.

Mix together the fruit bits or raisins, soaking water, sugar, oil, salt, flour, and the nuts. Stir to blend. Add the cinnamon and almond extract if desired. The batter should be thick—to spoon rather than pour. If thin, add a small amount of flour.

Spoon the batter into the prepared cans. Fill between one-half to two-thirds full. Push the batter down into the bottom with a spatula. Bake 1 hour, or until a deep, dark brown.

Remove the breads from the oven and allow to sit for 10 minutes before slipping them out of the containers. Let the breads cool completely on wire racks. When completely cooled, return the breads to the cans and cover with their plastic lids or wrap tightly in plastic.

Makes 2 loaves

Buttermilk–Brown Sugar Pound Cake ■ Chocolate Nut Torte ■ Flourless Chocolate Cake ■ German Chocolate Cake ■ Crème Anglaise ■ Vision Spice Cake with Mocha Buttercream ■ Pantry Fudge ■ Christmas Almond Toffee ■ Nut Brittle for Grown-Ups ■ Toasted Pecan Bars ■ Kahlúa Brownie Triangles ■ Butterscotch Pennies ■ Zebra Cookies ■ Grand-mother Kreiser's Meringue Cookies ■ Cardamom Wedding Cookies ■ Cranberry Softies ■ Sam's Marbled Biscotti ■ Pumpkin Drops ■ Chocolate

DESSERTS

Banana Pudding ■ Floating Islands (Oeufs à la Neige) ■ Marianna Reed's Cuban Flan ■ Rodney's Simply Delicious Baked Vanilla Custard ■ Simple One-Step Panettone ■ Lemon Poppy Seed Scones ■ Margaret Ann's Gingerbread Scones ■ Pistachio Nut Tea Bread ■ Carrot-Applesauce Muffins ■ Chocolate Meringue Pie ■ Coconut Custard Pie ■ No-Bake Refrigerator Cheesecake Pie ■ Sweet Potato Pecan Pie ■ Caramel Brown Sugar Pie ■ Lu Len's Beginner's Piecrust ■ Sweet Double Piecrust

THE DESSERT PANTRY is the easiest. With flour, baking powder, baking soda, salt, sugar, butter or shortening, and eggs, there are dozens of wonderful recipes to be had. Add chocolate, cocoa extracts, dried fruits, nuts, flavorings, and ingenuity and you will find the combinations endless. Dried milk can pull you out of a tight spot, as can the long-life shelf milk. Sweetened condensed and evaporated milks and dried buttermilk powder play important roles as well.

There is just one place to be unforgiving in the dessert pantry; try to get the best equipment you can—a good metal pie pan is a million times better than a flimsy aluminum foil one. A good rolling pin, mixer, baking sheet, and cake pan will make an enormous difference in your baking. Oven and candy thermometers are imperative. So too are spatulas, wooden spoons, and measuring cups and spoons. This is one place to avoid skimping.

If you don't have the right size pan, consider cutting a larger one down in size using aluminum foil as a divider, then placing another pan against the aluminum foil to hold it up. Alternately, double or divide a recipe. However, do this carefully; it is difficult to increase a baking recipe by more than one multiple or one division, and even that is tricky. Write down the new quantities to make sure all ingredients are proportional.

Most of these recipes will stun your family and guests when they figure you didn't have to go out and buy a thing.

BUTTERMILK–BROWN SUGAR POUND CAKE

Among desserts, pound cakes have one of the largest followings. Once the ingredients are combined and in the oven, pound cake takes little attention, and they are *so* good! This is a light batter that is enhanced by brown sugar and buttermilk. Serve with afternoon tea (it toasts beautifully) or with fresh berries and ice cream for a great summertime treat. It freezes well for 3 months.

1 8-ounce package cream cheese, softened

$\frac{1}{2}$ cup (1 stick) butter, softened

$1\frac{1}{2}$ cups granulated sugar

1 cup packed brown sugar

6 eggs

3 cups all-purpose flour

$\frac{1}{2}$ teaspoon baking powder

$\frac{1}{2}$ teaspoon baking soda

$\frac{1}{2}$ teaspoon salt

1 cup fresh or reconstituted powdered buttermilk

1 tablespoon vanilla extract

Preheat the oven to 325°F. Grease and flour a 10-inch tube pan or two 9 × 5 × 3-inch loaf pans. Set aside.

In a large bowl, beat the cream cheese, butter, granulated sugar, and brown sugar with an electric mixer until light, about 3 minutes. Add the eggs, one at a time, beating for 1 minute after each addition. Sift together the flour, baking powder, baking soda, and salt. Combine the buttermilk and vanilla. Add the flour mixture, alternating with the buttermilk mixture, to the butter-egg mixture, beginning and ending with the dry ingredients. Pour into the prepared pan and bake until a wooden toothpick inserted into the center comes out clean, 1 to 1$\frac{1}{4}$ hours. Cool in the pan for 10 minutes on a wire rack, then remove from the pan and cool completely.

Serves 8

Makes 1 10-inch round or 2 loaf cakes

CHOCOLATE NUT TORTE

This nutty chocolate torte is full of flavor and crunch. I have a few friends who can't eat wheat, so I serve this to them when they feel deprived of cakes and pies. We like it with the ½ cup sugar, but if you have a sweet tooth, go ahead and add the larger amount. If desperate, use all semi-sweet chocolate and be sure to use only ½ cup sugar.

This cake is so rich it should serve 8 to 10, but with any chocolate lover this is debatable. Let your conscience be your guide. The torte can be frozen for 3 months.

TOASTING NUTS
Toasting nuts intensi-fies the flavor desirable for certain recipes. However, they burn very easily due to their fat content. Spread them out on a baking sheet and toast in the oven at 350° F. for a couple min-utes. Keep an eye on them and don't scorch them. They're done when they are golden and fragrant. An easy alternative is to spread 1 cup out in a single layer on a flat microwave-safe plate and cook for 3 minutes at regular power. Shake them and stir them up, and cook for 3 minutes longer.

8 ounces hazelnuts, pecans, or walnuts, toasted
¼ to ½ cup granulated sugar
½ cup (1 stick) butter
3 ounces unsweetened chocolate
3 ounces semisweet chocolate
5 eggs, separated

Pinch of salt
Confectioners' sugar or cocoa powder, for sifting

TOPPING
1 cup heavy cream
3 tablespoons confectioners' sugar

Preheat the oven to 350° F. Butter or oil a 9-inch round cake pan or spring-form pan. Line the bottom of the pan with wax paper and butter or oil it.

Place half the cooled nuts in the bowl of a food processor, nut grinder, or blender and process just until finely ground. Chop the rest into small chunks. Set aside.

In a large heavy saucepan, place the sugar, butter, and unsweetened and semisweet chocolates. Stir over low heat until just melted and well mixed. The mixture will be grainy. Cool for 5 to 7 minutes. Whisk the egg yolks into the chocolate. Add the ground nuts. In a separate bowl, beat the egg whites with the salt until stiff peaks form. Gently fold the beaten whites into the chocolate mixture in 3 batches.

Pour the batter into the prepared pan and bake 30 to 35 minutes. The top of the cake will looked cracked and dry. Cool in the pan on a wire rack.

Remove the cake from the pan and set on a platter. Sift confectioners' sugar over the top. If desired, beat the cream with the confectioners' sugar until stiff and serve with the torte.

Serves 8 to 10

FLOURLESS CHOCOLATE CAKE

COCOA FOR CHOCOLATE
To use cocoa instead of chocolate, substitute 3 level tablespoons of cocoa and 1 tablespoon shortening or oil for each one ounce square of unsweetened baking chocolate.

Chocolate, butter, and eggs combine to make a mousse so rich and thick it can be sliced and served like a cake. It may be halved and cooked in a smaller pan; reduce the cooking time to 15 minutes. This is not for the weak of heart! This cake freezes for up to 3 months.

1 pound semisweet chocolate
10 tablespoons (1¼ sticks) butter,
* softened*

4 large eggs
1 tablespoon sugar
½ to 1 cup heavy cream, whipped

Preheat the oven to 375°F. Butter the bottom and sides of an 8-inch springform pan. Line the bottom of the pan with wax paper and butter the paper.

In a large heavy saucepan, melt the chocolate and butter over very low heat. Set aside to cool.

Whisk the eggs and sugar with an electric mixer until light and tripled in volume, about 5 minutes. The mixture should leave a ribbon when the beaters are lifted. Fold one-third of the egg mixture into the chocolate, and then fold the chocolate mixture back into the remaining egg mixture. Place the mixture in the prepared pan. Bake until set, 15 to 25 minutes. Cool on a wire rack.

Remove the sides of the pan and invert onto a serving dish. Peel off the paper. Chill and serve with whipped cream.

Serves 10 to 12

GERMAN CHOCOLATE CAKE

For the longest time I thought this cake originated in Germany. Then one day I found a recipe on the back of a German's Chocolate package and the light went on! Whatever the origin, this is now an all-American, grassroots classic and I like it—but, of course, I've changed it by adding more chocolate and some pecans. If this is a family favorite in your house, be sure to add sweet chocolate, coconut, and evaporated milk to your baking pantry list. You can use canned or frozen coconut.

½ cup boiling water

6 ounces sweet chocolate, chopped

1 cup (2 sticks) butter, at room
  temperature

2 cups sugar

4 egg yolks

1 teaspoon vanilla extract

2½ cups all-purpose flour

1 teaspoon baking soda

½ teaspoon salt

1 cup fresh or reconstituted powdered
  buttermilk

4 egg whites, stiffly beaten

1 cup roughly chopped pecans or walnuts

COCONUT-PECAN
FROSTING

¾ cup evaporated milk

1½ cups sugar

4 egg yolks, slightly beaten

¾ cup (1½ sticks) butter

1½ teaspoons vanilla extract

1 7-ounce package flaked coconut

1½ cups chopped pecans

Preheat the oven to 350°F. Butter 3 round layer pans, 8 or 9 × 1½ inches, or 2 square pans, 8 × 8 × 2 inches or 9 × 9 × 2 inches. Line the bottoms of the pans with wax paper and butter the paper.

Pour the boiling water over the chocolate, stirring until the chocolate is melted; set aside to cool.

In a large mixer bowl, beat the butter and sugar together until light. Add the egg yolks, 1 at a time, beating after each addition. Slowly blend in the melted chocolate and the vanilla. Blend together the flour, baking soda, and salt and mix into the butter, alternating with the buttermilk, beating after each addition until the batter is smooth. Fold in the egg whites and then the pecans. Divide the batter among the pans.

CHOCOLATE
There are many types of chocolate available, all with different names and characteristics. But the majority of chocolates fall into one of three categories: unsweetened, sweetened, and milk chocolate.

Semisweet and sweet chocolates all started as unsweetened chocolate and had sugar added at some point in their processing. (The amount of cocoa fat and quality of cocoa beans can vary considerably, as can any other flavorings that have been added.) I have used unsweetened chocolate when desperate in place of semisweet and bittersweet chocolate with varying degrees of success. Sugar adds structure to baking, so it can really change a recipe.

Chocolate should be stored between 68 and 78 degrees in a l dark place. You may refrigerate it if you know you will be gone a long time, but it will "sweat" moisture when it is brought to room temperature. Chocolate also acquires a chalky white exterior called "bloom" when it is kept at too warm temperatures. Either way, it can still be used for cooking.

Bake until the top springs back when touched lightly: 8–inch round layers, 35 to 40 minutes; 9–inch round layers, 30 to 35 minutes; 8–inch squares, 45 to 50 minutes; or 9–inch squares, 40 to 45 minutes. Cool in the pans on wire racks. Remove from the pans.

To make the frosting, combine the evaporated milk, sugar, egg yolks, and butter in a very heavy saucepan. Cook and stir over medium heat until thick, about 12 minutes. It should have come to a gentle boil. Stir in the vanilla, coconut, and pecans. Beat with a mixer until thick and cold enough to spread.

Put strips of wax paper around the outside edge of a serving plate. Put the bottom layer of the cake on top, with the paper extending out. Spread the frosting on each layer and on the top of the cake. Remove the wax paper.

Makes 1 cake

CRÈME ANGLAISE

This very basic light custard sauce, named for the English, is easily varied. It freezes to become ice cream; with the addition of gelatin it's a bavarois; with chocolate it's a chocolate sauce; and with butter it's a rich butter cream.

1½ cups milk
4 egg yolks
½ cup sugar

¼ cup cold milk or heavy cream
½ to 1 teaspoon vanilla extract

Heat the 1½ cups milk until small bubbles form at the edges of the pan. In a bowl, combine the yolks and sugar and beat until thick. Transfer to a heavy saucepan and slowly pour the hot milk over the yolk mixture. Cook for a few minutes over medium heat, stirring with a wooden spoon until the mixture coats the spoon like a sheer fabric—about 180°F. on an instant-reading thermometer. A finger run down the back of the spoon should leave a separation. Don't overcook it or the eggs will be scrambled. Stir in the cold milk and vanilla and immediately pour through a fine strainer into another bowl. Refrigerate, covered with plastic wrap.

Makes 2 cups

VISION SPICE CAKE WITH MOCHA BUTTERCREAM

Margaret Ann created this one day when Ray and Patti had birthdays the same week. We call it the vision cake because she developed it on National Dessert Day and "had a vision" of it on her way to work. Fortunately, we had everything she needed to realize that vision in the baking pantry, and you probably do too. The cake and the buttercream freeze well, up to 3 months, but the buttercream must be brought completely to room temperature before using if frozen separately. Beat it for 1 to 2 minutes to fluff it up.

EGGS GUIDELINES
Whenever possible buy grade AA eggs. They will last longer and both the white and yolk are firmer and more distinct. Large eggs are 2 ounces, with the white a bit more than an ounce and the yolk a bit less. Extra large eggs are 2¼ ounces and medium ones are 1¾. If you need to substitute, use a liquid measuring cup to determine if you have an equal amount. Egg whites freeze well. Yolks do freeze, but I find them generally a nuisance and so rarely bother.

3¾ cups cake flour
1 tablespoon ground cinnamon
½ teaspoon ground cloves
1 teaspoon ground allspice
1 teaspoon ground nutmeg
½ teaspoon salt
1½ cups sugar
1 cup buttermilk
1½ teaspoons baking soda
1 cup (2 sticks) butter, at room temperature

4 eggs, separated
2 cups raisins, plumped in hot water for 20 minutes, drained, and patted dry

BUTTERCREAM
4 egg whites, at room temperature
1 cup sugar
1¾ cups (3½ sticks) butter, softened
2 ounces unsweetened chocolate, melted
1 tablespoon instant coffee, dissolved in 3 to 4 tablespoons boiling water

Preheat the oven to 350°F. Grease and flour 2 9-inch round cake pans. Line the bottoms with wax paper and grease and flour the paper.

In a large mixer bowl, combine 3½ cups flour, the cinnamon, cloves, allspice, nutmeg, salt, and sugar. Mix at low speed until combined. In a mixing cup, combine the buttermilk with the baking soda. Add the butter and ¼ cup of the buttermilk to the dry ingredients and beat on low speed until moist. Combine the egg yolks with the remaining buttermilk and add this mixture to the batter, one-third at a time, mixing at high speed for 30 to 45 seconds after each addition. Toss the raisins with the remaining ¼ cup of flour and fold them into the batter.

In another mixer bowl, beat the egg whites to soft peaks, then fold them into the batter. Divide the batter between the 2 pans and bake 30 to 40 minutes. A toothpick inserted in the center will come out clean. Turn onto a wire rack and let cool completely.

For the buttercream, combine the egg whites and sugar in a large mixer bowl and set the bowl in a larger bowl of warm water. Stir until the sugar has dissolved. Remove the bowl from the warm water. Beat the whites at high speed until stiff peaks form. Gradually beat in the softened butter, 1 to 2 tablespoons at a time, at medium-high speed. The mixture may look slightly curdled, but continue beating and it will thicken and smooth out. Add the melted chocolate and the coffee and beat again until smooth.

Spread the buttercream on the first layer, top with the second layer, and frost the top and sides, piping decoratively if desired. Keep cool or refrigerated.

Makes 1 2-layer 9-inch cake

PANTRY FUDGE

I devised this one day when I had to make a quick trip to the hospital to see my father and wanted something to win over the nurses. It can be placed in the freezer until hard.

1 12-ounce package semisweet chocolate chips
1 6-ounce package unsweetened chocolate
1 14-ounce can sweetened condensed milk (not evaporated milk)

Dash of salt
½ to 1 cup chopped pecans or walnuts
1 teaspoon orange extract

Line an 8- or 9-inch square pan with wax paper.

Melt the chocolates with the milk and salt in a heavy saucepan over low heat or in the microwave. Remove from the heat and stir in the nuts and orange extract. Spread evenly in the prepared pan. Chill 2 hours or place in the freezer until firm. Turn the fudge onto a cutting board, peel off the paper, and cut into squares. Store loosely covered at room temperature.

Makes 2 pounds

CHRISTMAS ALMOND TOFFEE

I love toffee, that delightful buttery candy full of nuts and topped with chocolate. This is faster to make than cookies—no in and out of the oven—although the caramel takes time on the front end. If your baking pantry is up to date you'll have all the ingredients at the ready to make up a few pounds for holiday gift giving.

ALMOND SUBSTITUTIONS
If a recipe calls for sliced almonds and you don't have any—substitute! The flavor would be the same if you used slivered. But do pay attention to texture: you may want to cook smaller, thinner sliced almonds less.

2 cups packed brown sugar
1 cup (2 sticks) butter
¼ cup water
1 tablespoon vanilla extract

½ teaspoon baking soda
1 12-ounce package chocolate chips
1½ cups sliced toasted almonds, coarsely
   chopped

Lightly grease a 10 × 15-inch baking sheet. Set aside.

In a large heavy saucepan, combine the brown sugar, butter, and water and bring slowly to the boil, stirring occasionally to prevent burning. Insert a candy thermometer and cook until the mixture reaches 285°F. (soft-crack stage). Remove from the heat and quickly stir in the vanilla and baking soda. Immediately pour onto the greased baking sheet.

Sprinkle the chocolate chips over the hot toffee. Let sit for 5 minutes, then spread evenly over the surface of the toffee with a spatula. Sprinkle the nuts evenly over the top. Cool completely. Break the hardened toffee into pieces and store in an airtight container.

Makes about 1½ pounds

NUT BRITTLE FOR GROWN-UPS

Here is another easy sweet to stir together when there are no munchies around. You probably have a can of mixed nuts stowed away for impromptu guests, and that is perfect for this. Of course, if money and calories are not an issue, why not macadamia nuts? Or any other nut, for that matter.

1 cup light corn syrup

2 cups sugar

¼ cup water

3 cups deluxe mixed nuts

¼ cup (½ stick) butter

½ teaspoon baking soda

2 teaspoons vanilla extract

Grease a 10 × 15-inch baking sheet with a lip.

In a large Dutch oven, combine the corn syrup, sugar, and water and stir to blend. Place over medium heat, bring to the boil, and stir until the sugar has dissolved. Continue cooking without stirring until the mixture reaches 300° F. on a candy thermometer. Remove from the heat and stir in the nuts, butter, baking soda, and vanilla.

Working quickly, pour the mixture onto the baking sheet and spread into as thin a layer as possible. Allow the candy to cool completely, then break it up into bite-size pieces. Store in a tightly covered container.

Makes 2 pounds

TOASTED PECAN BARS

Bar cookies are such a pleasure to make. No in and out of the oven for sheet after sheet of cookies, yet you wind up with a gracious plenty. These use a modest assortment of items from the baking pantry, plus plenty of nuts. You can, of course, use whatever variety you've got in sufficient quantity. They freeze for 2 months.

CRUST

1½ cups all-purpose flour

¾ cup chopped toasted pecans (see Note)

1 teaspoon baking powder

½ teaspoon salt

¾ cup (1½ sticks) butter, softened

½ cup packed light brown sugar

FILLING

½ cup heavy cream

2 eggs, beaten

½ cup light corn syrup

⅓ cup packed light brown sugar

¼ cup (½ stick) butter, melted

1 tablespoon vanilla extract

1 cup chopped pecans

Preheat the oven to 375°F. Lightly butter a 9 × 13-inch baking dish.

In a mixing bowl, toss together the flour, pecans, baking powder, and salt. In a separate bowl, beat together the butter and brown sugar with an electric mixer for 1 minute. Add the flour mixture and stir until thoroughly blended. Spread about half of this dough in the prepared dish, then press it into the bottom and only slightly up the sides. Bake 20 minutes. Cool on a rack for 15 minutes. Lower the oven temperature to 350°F.

In a large bowl, combine the cream, eggs, corn syrup, brown sugar, and butter. Continue to mix until the sugar is evenly dispersed. Stir in the vanilla and the pecans. Pour over the cooled crust. Sprinkle with the remaining crumb mixture and bake 40 minutes. Cool in the pan for several hours before cutting into bars.

Makes 36

NOTE: *To toast pecans, spread the nuts on a baking sheet and toast in a 350°F oven for 8 to 10 minutes, or until golden and fragrant. Alternately, toast in the microwave according to microwave directions.*

BROWN SUGAR
Brown sugars are made of white granulated sugar to which a dark syrup or molasses has been added. The color and flavor of the sugar vary according to which colorant is used. The darker they are, the stronger they flavor, but they can almost always be used interchangeably in recipes, which is why I rarely specify light or dark in my recipes—it's a matter of personal preference.

KAHLÚA BROWNIE TRIANGLES

SPIRITED FLAVORING
Even if you don't serve alcohol with meals, it's useful to keep a variety of spirits on hand to flavor foods. The alcohol burns off if boiled sufficiently, leaving only the subtle tang and smoky flavor of the spirit. While many wines and spirits can be used interchangeably—dry vermouth for white wine, cognac for Armagnac, for example—the distinctive flavors of dry and sweet Madeira sherry and Marsala, brandy, Grand Marnier or other orange liqueur, and Kahlúa make them worth having in the liquor cabinet to flavor desserts, sauces, macerate fruit, and more. However, it's usually just fine to substitute broth, cider, or even water, plus a tablespoon or so of a good vinegar, for wine in most recipes.

These sinfully rich brownies are a snap to make. The untraditional shape and the white chocolate put these brownies a step above the rest. The addition of the dark corn syrup helps to make this sweet treat delightfully moist and chewy, the way I remember them. These freeze for 2 months.

1 cup (2 sticks) butter

8 ounces unsweetened chocolate

6 eggs

1½ cups sugar

1 cup packed light or dark brown sugar

½ cup dark corn syrup

1½ cups all-purpose flour

½ teaspoon instant coffee granules

½ teaspoon baking soda

½ teaspoon salt

1 teaspoon vanilla extract

2 tablespoons Kahlúa or other coffee liqueur

2 cups chopped pecans

½ cup melted white chocolate

Preheat the oven to 350°F. Grease and flour a 15 × 10-inch jelly roll pan.

In a medium saucepan, combine the butter and chocolate. Heat over low heat until melted and smooth, stirring occasionally. Cool.

In a large bowl, beat together the eggs and sugars. Beat in the cooled chocolate mixture. Add the corn syrup, flour, instant coffee, baking soda, salt, vanilla, and Kahlúa and beat until well blended. Stir in the pecans.

Spread the batter evenly in the pan and bake 25 to 30 minutes. Do not overbake—the brownies should be moist in the center. Cool in the pan. Drizzle the brownies with melted white chocolate. Cut the cooled brownies into triangles or diamond shapes.

Makes 48 1½-inch triangles

BUTTERSCOTCH PENNIES

This recipe and the next are adapted from *365 Great Cookies and Brownies* by Joanne Lamb Hayes and Bonnie Tandy Leblang. Joanne showed these cookies off on my TV show.

¾ cup packed light or dark brown sugar
¾ cup (1½ sticks) butter, softened
1 teaspoon vanilla extract

1¾ cups all-purpose flour
½ teaspoon baking powder
¼ teaspoon salt

In a large bowl or mixer, beat together the brown sugar, butter, and vanilla on medium speed until well blended. In a medium bowl, combine the flour, baking powder, and salt. Beat the dry ingredients into the sugar-butter mixture until smooth, scraping down the sides of the bowl with a rubber spatula.

Divide the dough into 2 equal pieces. With the palms of your hands, roll each piece into a 10 × ¾-inch rope. Wrap the ropes in wax paper and refrigerate for at least 3 hours.

When ready to bake the cookies, preheat the oven to 350°F. Lightly grease several cookie sheets. Thinly slice the dough crosswise into ⅛-inch rounds. Place the rounds 1 inch apart on the cookie sheets. Bake until firm and very lightly browned on the edges, about 8 to 10 minutes. Remove the cookies to a wire rack and let cool completely. Store in a tightly covered container.

Makes about 13 dozen

ZEBRA COOKIES

⅔ cup sugar
½ cup (1 stick) butter, softened
1 egg
2 teaspoons vanilla extract
1¾ cups all-purpose flour

½ teaspoon baking powder
¼ teaspoon salt
2 1-ounce squares unsweetened
   chocolate, melted

In a large bowl, beat the sugar and butter with an electric mixer on medium speed until well blended. Beat in the egg and vanilla until light.

Beat in the flour mixed with baking powder and salt until the dough is smooth, scraping down the sides of the bowl frequently with a rubber spatula.

Shape one half of the dough into a square roll, 2 inches on a side; be sure to make sides flat. Place the remaining dough in a small bowl. Stir in the chocolate until well blended. Shape the chocolate dough into a square roll, 2 inches to a side. Wrap and refrigerate at least 3 hours or up to 3 days.

When ready to bake cookies, preheat the oven to 350°F. Slice both pieces of dough lengthwise to make 4 long slices. Reassemble rolls alternating chocolate and light doughs. Slice rolls crosswise to make ¼-inch thick cookies. Place cookies 2 inches apart on lightly greased cookie sheets. Bake 12 to 15 minutes, or until firm and very lightly browned on the edges. Remove the cookies to a wire rack and let cool completely. Store in an airtight container.

Makes about 4 dozen

GRANDMOTHER KREISER'S MERINGUE COOKIES

The success of meringues is very weather dependent. (My great-uncle Harry's wife, called Grandmother Kreiser, felt they were better when stabilized with vinegar.) Meringues are difficult to make in humid weather. They are really "dried," not baked, and technically should be white when done, although frankly I sometimes don't mind the light brown, chewy product of a humid day. Traditionally, meringues are several inches around, with several levels, but I like the little ones that look like large candy kisses.

3 egg whites
Pinch of salt
¾ cup sugar

½ teaspoon vanilla extract
½ teaspoon vinegar

Preheat the oven to 225°F. Line a cookie sheet with wax paper.

Beat the egg whites and salt until stiff. Fold in the sugar, vanilla, and vinegar. Pipe or drop in 1- or 2-inch rounds, preferably pointed, onto the prepared cookie sheet. Bake until firm, 1 to 2 hours.

Makes 8 large or 24 small cookies

CARDAMOM WEDDING COOKIES

These crispy cookies explode with flavor as they break into pieces in your mouth. Grating the citrus takes the most time—the rest is easy and produces great results. They are dusted a pretty white and ideal for receptions. My friend Amanda Brown Olmstead, mother of my goddaughter, served these at the party she had for me after my wedding. They were *perfect*. They freeze for up to 3 months.

1 cup (2 sticks) butter, softened
2/3 cup confectioners' sugar
2 teaspoons vanilla extract
Grated peel (no white attached) of
    1 lemon
Grated peel (no white attached) of
    1 orange

1 cup all-purpose flour
3/4 cup whole wheat flour
1/2 cup cornstarch
2 teaspoons ground cardamom
1 cup finely ground almonds or pecans
1 to 2 cups sifted confectioners' sugar,
    for dusting

Preheat the oven to 325°F.

In a mixer bowl, beat the butter and confectioners' sugar together until light. Beat in the vanilla and lemon and orange peels. Sift together the flours, cornstarch, and cardamom and add to the butter mixture. Mix at low speed until almost combined, then add the ground nuts and mix until combined. Shape into balls the size of a nickel and place on an ungreased baking sheet. Bake until the bottoms are lightly browned, 20 to 25 minutes. Transfer to a wire rack to cool for 5 minutes, then roll in sifted confectioners' sugar and let finish cooling completely on a rack. Roll again in confectioners' sugar and store in an airtight container.

Makes 36

CRANBERRY SOFTIES

Soft with tangy bits of fresh or frozen cranberries and flavored with orange peel, these cookies are a pleasant diversion. We developed them in a search for soft cookies, which are the only kind my dad can eat. When I make them for him I omit the nuts, which he has trouble chewing. They freeze well for up to 3 months.

1/4 cup (1/2 stick) butter, at room
    temperature
3/4 cup packed light brown sugar
1 egg
1 teaspoon vanilla extract
1 tablespoon grated orange peel (no white
    attached)

Pinch of salt
1 1/2 cups all-purpose flour
1/2 teaspoon baking soda
1/2 cup chopped walnuts or pecans
3/4 cup chopped fresh or thawed frozen
    cranberries

Preheat the oven to 375°F. Grease 2 baking sheets.

In a medium bowl, beat together the butter, brown sugar, egg, vanilla, orange peel, and salt until light. Add the flour and baking soda, beating until well blended. Stir in the walnuts by hand, then carefully fold in the cranberries.

Drop the batter by teaspoonfuls at least 2 inches apart onto the baking sheets. Bake until golden, 10 to 12 minutes. With a wide spatula, immediately remove the cookies to a wire rack to cool. Store in an airtight container.

Makes 48 1 3/4-inch cookies

SAM'S MARBLED BISCOTTI

Sam is a tall and lovely young woman who briefly apprenticed for me. She had enormous baking talent and tested and retested this recipe. Biscotti (which means twice-baked) are a marvelously adaptable kind of recipe, receptive to any number of ingredients you're likely to have around. Omit the cocoa and coffee if you prefer. Substitute pistachios or hazelnuts for the almonds, or use fennel or anise seeds soaked in a bit of sweet vermouth. With so many options, you can make these anytime.

2 to 2½ cups all-purpose flour (see Note)

1 cup sugar

2 teaspoons baking powder

2 large eggs

2 large egg whites

2 teaspoons vanilla extract

2 tablespoons unsweetened cocoa powder

1 tablespoon instant coffee granules

4 teaspoons boiling water

1 cup whole almonds, toasted

1 teaspoon almond extract

1 cup chocolate chips

Preheat the oven to 325°F. Lightly grease a large cookie sheet and set aside.

In a large bowl, stir together 2 cups of the flour, the sugar, and baking powder. In a small bowl, mix together the eggs, egg whites, and vanilla. Add the egg mixture to the dry ingredients and stir until smooth. Divide the dough in half and place each half in a mixing bowl.

In a small bowl, combine the cocoa, coffee granules, and boiling water. Add the cocoa mixture to 1 bowl of dough and the almonds and almond extract to the other bowl. Refrigerate the doughs separately for 30 minutes, or until firm. Place the almond dough on a well-floured work surface and pat into a thin 6 × 12-inch rectangle. Form the chocolate dough into a 12-inch log and place on top of the almond rectangle. Fold the almond dough over the chocolate dough to form a log. Place the log on a cookie sheet and pat into a rectangle 1 inch thick.

Bake until firm, 20 to 25 minutes. Transfer the log to a wire rack and cool 5 minutes. Reduce the oven temperature to 300°F. Using a serrated knife, cut the dough into ½-inch-thick slices. Stand the slices upright on the baking sheet and return to the oven for 25 to 30 minutes, until crisp and dry. Cool completely on wire racks.

Melt the chocolate chips in a small saucepan over low heat. Using a pastry brush, paint melted chocolate onto 1 end of the biscotti. Place on wax paper until the chocolate hardens. Store in airtight containers.

Makes 15

NOTE: *If you only have cake flour or other soft wheat all-purpose flour available, you will need an extra ½ cup or so of flour to reduce the stickiness and make the dough manageable.*

PUMPKIN DROPS

After the holidays I wind up with extra cans of pumpkin as well as nuts. Patti and Margaret Ann came up with this simple way to use up the "leftovers," winding up with a moist, chewy cookie. The cookies freeze for 2 to 3 months.

¾ cup (1½ sticks) butter, at room temperature
⅔ cup packed light brown sugar
2 eggs
1½ teaspoons vanilla extract
1 cup canned or cooked fresh pumpkin puree

2 cups all-purpose flour
½ teaspoon baking powder
½ teaspoon baking soda
Pinch of salt
2½ teaspoons pumpkin pie spice
1 cup chocolate chips
1 cup chopped walnuts or pecans

Preheat the oven to 375°F.

In a large bowl, beat together the butter, brown sugar, eggs, and vanilla until light. Beat in the pumpkin. Add the flour, baking powder, baking soda, salt, and pumpkin pie spice, beating until blended. Stir in the chocolate chips and walnuts. Drop teaspoonfuls of the batter 2 inches apart onto ungreased baking sheets. Bake until the edges are golden, 10 to 12 minutes. Transfer the cookies from the baking sheets to a wire rack to cool.

Makes about 80 1½-inch cookies

CHOCOLATE BANANA PUDDING

I love banana pudding—homey, simple, gooey, rich, and familiar. Add chocolate and it's over the top! If, like me, you freeze bananas when they start to turn brown, you can use those in this recipe. I've also made it with dried bananas.

1 cup plus 2 tablespoons sugar
¼ cup all-purpose flour
Pinch of salt
3 cups milk
8 egg yolks
1 tablespoon vanilla extract

2 ounces bittersweet chocolate, melted
1 12-ounce box vanilla wafers
8 bananas, sliced
6 egg whites
½ ounce grated semisweet chocolate

Preheat the oven to 375°F.

In a large heavy saucepan, stir together the 1 cup sugar, flour, and salt. Gradually whisk in the milk and heat to 170°F. In a small bowl, beat the egg yolks briefly and whisk in some of the hot milk. Pour this mixture back into the saucepan, bring to the boil over low heat, stirring constantly, and cook slowly until the custard is thick. Remove from the heat and stir in the vanilla. Stir in the melted chocolate until well blended.

Line the bottom and sides of a 4-quart ovenproof serving dish with vanilla wafers. Cover with a layer of bananas. Cover the bananas with a layer of custard. Continue layering until the bowl is full, ending with custard.

In a separate bowl, beat the egg whites until soft peaks form. Add the 2 tablespoons sugar and beat to stiff, shiny peaks. Fold in the grated chocolate, spread the mixture over the top of the pudding, and bake until browned, 10 to 15 minutes. Serve hot.

Serves 10 to 12

STORING FRUITS

One of the first rules is to keep different fruits separate, with the exception of tomatoes and apples. The apples will help ripen the tomatoes. Bananas, however, turn brown when in contact with tomatoes or apples and do much better on their own. Most bananas and tomatoes are picked and shipped green and need ripening—they should not be refrigerated. Apples, pears, and peaches, on the other hand, will never ripen more than they are when you purchase them. They should be refrigerated for best results. Apples and pears can be kept a long time in cold storage or refrigerated.

FLOATING ISLANDS
(*OEUFS À LA NEIGE*)

These delicate, snowy puffs float on a cool custard and are topped with streams of golden caramel. They cause exclamations of praise. Who would know all you had in the house was milk, sugar, vanilla, and eggs?! To make tender floating islands, the egg whites should be poached in water that doesn't exceed a temperature of 170°F.

3 egg whites
¼ teaspoon cream of tartar
Pinch of salt
½ cup sugar
1 recipe Crème Anglaise (page 171)

CARAMEL
½ cup sugar
¼ cup water
¼ cup light corn syrup

Beat the whites with the cream of tartar and salt by hand or with an electric mixer until shiny and glossy. Fold in the sugar.

Meanwhile, heat a deep sauté pan of water to a temperature of 170°F. Using an ice-cream scoop or 2 large metal spoons, form ovals of whites, using your finger to get the "egg" as round as possible. Gently drop the "egg" into the water. Poach 1 to 2 minutes, until the "eggs" turn over when prodded gently. Poach on the second side, then lift out with a slotted spoon or spatula onto wax paper or brown paper to drain.

Pour the chilled Crème Anglaise into a serving dish with a rim. Gently arrange the little islands on the sauce. Refrigerate while you prepare the caramel.

Heat the sugar with the water and corn syrup in a heavy pan until the sugar dissolves. Do not allow to boil before the sugar dissolves or it may crystallize. Bring to the boil and boil rapidly until the syrup is a golden caramel color. Stop the boiling at once by dipping the bottom of the pan in a pan of cold water.

Using a fork or whisk, drizzle the hot caramel over the "eggs."

Serves 8

MARIANNA REED'S CUBAN FLAN

Marianna was a cooking student of mine from Miami. She declared her flan from sweetened condensed milk as good as anyone's, so we tried it. Sure enough, it was! I always keep sweetened condensed milk around for quickie key lime pies, but now I have another great reason. It's thick, smooth, rich, and not too sweet. If you have no regular milk, reconstituted dry milk may be used, or another can of condensed, which will make it sweeter.

1 cup sugar

¼ cup water

1 14-ounce can sweetened condensed milk

1⅓ cups milk

6 egg yolks

2 teaspoons vanilla extract

Preheat the oven to 325°F.

Melt the sugar in the water in a small saucepan over low heat, brushing the sides of the pan with a wet brush. Do not boil. When dissolved, increase the heat and boil without stirring until the liquid turns golden caramel. Carefully pour into a warm 1-quart soufflé dish, turning the dish to coat the bottom and lower sides. Lightly whisk together the condensed milk, regular milk, egg yolks, and vanilla and pour carefully over the caramel in the soufflé dish so it doesn't foam.

Place a kitchen towel in the bottom of a roasting pan with sides. Place the soufflé dish on the towel in the middle of the pan. Carefully pour enough hot water into the pan to come halfway up the sides of the soufflé dish. Place in the middle of the oven and bake until set, about 1 hour. Carefully remove the pan from the oven and remove the soufflé dish from the pan. Cool slightly. Cover with plastic wrap, refrigerate, and chill completely. Just before serving, place a shallow serving plate on top of the soufflé dish and invert the dish so that the custard unmolds. The caramel will form a topping and sauce. Serve chilled.

Serves 6

RODNEY'S SIMPLY DELICIOUS BAKED VANILLA CUSTARD

When my friend Alma returned home from a hospital stay, she fantasized about a delicate, smooth baked custard like she had as a child. Rodney, one of my apprentices, fixed her this and she ate one serving warm from the oven—the first thing she'd eaten all of in a month. The rest she finished off, chilled, later in the day. It is truly delicious, smooth, light—an example of a perfect, simple food that is just waiting to be thrown together from your kitchen staples.

2³⁄₄ cups milk
¹⁄₄ cup sugar
1 vanilla bean or 2 teaspoons vanilla extract

3 egg yolks
1 whole egg

Preheat the oven to 350°F.

Place the milk, sugar, and vanilla bean if using into a 2-quart saucepan and heat until tiny bubbles appear around the edge of the pan. With a wooden spoon, beat together the egg yolks and egg until light in color. Remove the vanilla pod if used from the milk and slowly whisk the milk into the eggs. (If using vanilla extract, stir into the mixture at this point.) Carefully strain the mixture into either 4 1-cup ovenproof earthenware dishes or 1 4-cup ovenproof earthenware dish. Cover tightly with a lid or aluminum foil.

Place a kitchen towel in the bottom of a roasting pan with sides. Put the dish or dishes on the towel and add enough hot water to come halfway up the sides of the dish being used. Place the pan in the middle of the hot oven and cook until set, 12 minutes for 1-cup dishes or 30 minutes for a 4-cup dish. Remove from the oven and uncover immediately. The custard may be eaten warm or chilled.

Serves 4 (1-cup servings) or 8 (¹⁄₂-cup servings)

SIMPLE ONE-STEP PANETTONE

Panettone is a traditional Italian bread served at the holidays. Because it uses readily available pantry items, I think it should be served year-round with tea or as an afternoon treat. It is rather cakelike and is usually made with yeast and left to rise. To simplify things I've come up with a quick bread batter, which I bake in a cleaned coffee can to simulate the familiar conical shape.

2 eggs

½ cup sugar

½ cup (1 stick) butter, melted and cooled

1 teaspoon grated lemon peel (no white attached)

1 teaspoon vanilla extract

1 teaspoon lemon extract

3 cups all-purpose flour

2 teaspoons baking powder

½ teaspoon salt

1 cup buttermilk

½ cup slivered almonds

½ cup golden raisins

¼ cup chopped mixed dried fruits

Preheat the oven to 325°F. Grease a clean, empty 1-pound coffee can. Line the bottom with a piece of wax paper cut to fit and grease the paper.

In a large bowl, beat the eggs and sugar until thick and pale yellow, about 5 minutes. Beat in the melted butter, lemon peel, and vanilla and lemon extracts. In a small bowl, mix the flour, baking powder, and salt and blend into the creamed mixture alternately with the buttermilk. Stir in the almonds, raisins, and dried fruit. Pour the mixture into the prepared can and place on a baking sheet. Bake 55 to 60 minutes, or until the bread is well browned and a toothpick inserted in the center comes out clean. Cool the bread in the can for 10 minutes, then turn it out onto a rack to finish cooling. You may have to cut out the bottom of the can to push out the cake. To serve, cut into slices or wedges.

Makes 1 loaf

LEMON POPPY SEED SCONES

Ideal for brunch or tea, these slightly sweet, crunchy scones are a hit by themselves or served split with butter and your favorite honey, such as orange blossom. Your family and friends are certain to ask for seconds—maybe even thirds. For a crisper scone, allow about 1 inch between each shaped piece of dough when baking. These are best when served right out of the oven.

3 cups self-rising flour plus additional
    flour for shaping
½ cup sugar
½ teaspoon baking soda
½ teaspoon salt
1 teaspoon ground coriander
6 tablespoons (¾ stick) butter, chilled

1 egg
1 cup buttermilk
6 tablespoons poppy seeds
3 tablespoons grated lemon peel (no
    white attached)
½ cup confectioners' sugar (optional)

Preheat the oven to 500°F. Lightly grease a baking sheet.

In a large bowl, mix together 3 cups flour, the sugar, baking soda, salt, and coriander. With your fingers, 2 knives, or a pastry blender, cut in the chilled butter until the mixture resembles coarse meal. Mix the egg and buttermilk together and gently combine with the dry ingredients. Add the poppy seeds and lemon peel and stir until just moistened. Sprinkle additional flour over the surface of the dough, gently flip the dough over in the bowl, and dust this side with flour. Flour your hands, pinch off a piece of dough about the size of an egg, dip the wet end of dough into flour, and gently knead in your hand, shaping into a ball and then flattening slightly. Place the piece on the prepared pan so the scones are just touching. Repeat with the remaining dough. Bake 8 to 10 minutes, or until golden. Remove from the oven and place on a rack to cool slightly. Sprinkle with confectioners' sugar if desired and serve immediately.

Makes 18

MARGARET ANN'S GINGERBREAD SCONES

Just by themselves, as a tea cake, these are wonderful. Split them and fill with lemon curd or whipped cream and you're in a new world!

2 cups soft wheat flour
2 teaspoons baking powder
½ teaspoon salt
½ cup packed brown sugar
1 teaspoon ground ginger

½ teaspoon ground cinnamon
¼ teaspoon ground nutmeg
6 tablespoons (¾ stick) butter
1 cup cream, half-and-half, or evaporated
   milk

Preheat the oven to 400°F.

In a medium mixing bowl, combine the flour, baking powder, salt, brown sugar, ginger, cinnamon, and nutmeg. Cut in the butter with a pastry blender or 2 knives until the consistency of oatmeal. Make a well in the center and add the cream. Stir with a fork until just combined. Turn out onto a generously floured surface and divide the dough in half. Pat each half of the dough into a round ½ to ¾ inch thick. Cut each round into 6 wedges. Place the wedges on a lightly greased baking sheet and bake 15 to 18 minutes, or until golden. Cool on a rack. Serve warm.

Makes 12

LUMPY BROWN SUGAR

When brown sugar is too hard or dry to be pressed easily through a strainer or sieve, you can rehydrate and soften it. For a quick fix, put it on a paper towel in the microwave with a sliced apple and heat on High for a minute or two. If you have more time, put a damp (not sopping) paper towel or a slice of apple in the box, seal, and leave for 12 hours or overnight.

PISTACHIO NUT TEA BREAD

More a cake than a bread, this dessert bread has a definite orange tang. It freezes well for 2 months.

½ cup (1 stick) butter
1 cup sugar
2 eggs
¼ cup orange juice
Grated peel (no white attached) of 2 oranges

1½ cups self-rising flour
½ cup fresh or reconstituted powdered
   buttermilk
1 cup whole pistachios

PISTACHIOS

When a pistachio is ripe the shell splits open at one end, exposing the greenish colored nut. The shells are naturally light tan but are sometimes dyed red. Shelled pistachios are hard to find and not cheap, but are definitely a boon for bakers who value their manicures.

Preheat the oven to 350°F. Grease and flour a 9 × 5 × 3-inch loaf pan.

In a large mixing bowl, beat the butter and sugar until well blended. Beat in the eggs, orange juice, and peel until light. Add the flour, alternating with the buttermilk. Fold in the pistachios. Pour into the prepared pan and bake until a skewer inserted into the center comes out clean, about 1 hour.

Makes 1 loaf

CARROT-APPLESAUCE MUFFINS

These muffins are like miniature carrot cakes. The applesauce replaces most of the oil needed in the usual muffin recipe, providing the moisture and texture we expect in a breakfast bread. For mini muffins, reduce the baking time to 12 to 15 minutes.

1½ cups all-purpose flour
1 cup whole wheat flour
2 teaspoons baking powder
2 teaspoons baking soda
½ teaspoon salt
2 teaspoons ground cinnamon
1 teaspoon grated nutmeg
1 teaspoon ground cardamom
3 eggs

⅔ cup firmly packed light or dark brown sugar
2 teaspoons vanilla extract
⅓ cup vegetable oil
2 cups applesauce
3 cups grated carrots
1 cup raisins
Grated peel (no white attached) of 2 oranges

Preheat the oven to 350°F. Lightly spray muffin tins with nonstick cooking spray containing flour.

In a large bowl, sift together the flours, baking powder, baking soda, salt, cinnamon, nutmeg, and cardamom.

In a medium bowl, combine the eggs, brown sugar, and vanilla, mixing well. Stir in the vegetable oil, applesauce, carrots, raisins, and orange peel. Add to the flour and mix just until incorporated. Pour into the prepared muffin tins and bake until a tester inserted comes out clean, about 20 minutes. Cool 10 minutes on a wire rack, then invert and cool completely.

Makes 18 large or 36 small muffins

CHOCOLATE MERINGUE PIE

This pie is like an old-fashioned pudding your grandmother would have made. In fact, it is my father's favorite pie. This pie is just as good warm from the oven if family and friends have trouble waiting for it to chill but it will be runny, obviously! Be prepared to serve the pie the day it is made because it is almost impossible to keep it overnight once it is spied in the refrigerator—it is *that* good. If you don't have time to make the meringue, omit that step and spread with whipped cream—my dad likes that equally well. (The meringue cooking time does not cook the custard—it only browns the meringue.)

1¼ cups plus ⅓ cup sugar
½ teaspoon salt
½ cup cornstarch
¼ cup cocoa powder
5 eggs, separated

2½ cups milk
1 ounce semisweet chocolate
2 teaspoons vanilla extract
⅛ teaspoon ground cinnamon
1 prebaked 9-inch piecrust (page 197)

Preheat the oven to 350°F.

In a large heavy saucepan, thoroughly mix the 1¼ cups sugar, the salt, cornstarch, and cocoa. In a bowl, whisk together the egg yolks and milk. Add to the saucepan, whisking until the sugar has dissolved. Place over medium heat and cook, stirring occasionally until the custard is smooth, thick, and shiny, about 5 to 10 minutes. Boil the custard for 1 minute, stirring constantly to prevent sticking or scorching. Remove from the heat, add the semisweet chocolate, vanilla, and cinnamon and stir until the chocolate has melted. Place a sheet of plastic wrap directly on the custard so it does not form a skin.

Beat together the egg whites and remaining ⅓ cup sugar until the mixture forms soft peaks. Spoon the custard into the pie shell and top with the meringue, spreading it all the way to the edges. Bake until the top is golden brown, about 8 to 10 minutes. Remove from the oven, let it cool at room temperature for 1 hour, and then refrigerate until cold—approximately 3 hours before cutting.

Makes 1 9-inch pie

COCONUT CUSTARD PIE

Other than the coconut, everything in this recipe is basic, basic, basic. I keep a package of coconut in the freezer year-round because this recipe is a favorite.

COCONUT
Packaged coconut keeps well in the freezer. It is usually presweetened, but if it is too sweet for the recipe you are making or for your palette, rinse under running water and squeeze dry, a bit at a time, to remove the sugar.

1½ cups heavy cream
1¼ cups milk
¾ cup sugar
6 tablespoons cornstarch
2 large egg yolks
1 teaspoon vanilla extract
2 cups shredded coconut

MERINGUE TOPPING
5 large egg whites, at room temperature
½ cup sugar
½ teaspoon cream of tartar
1 prebaked piecrust (page 197)

Combine the cream and ½ cup of the milk in a saucepan with the sugar. Cook over low heat, stirring occasionally to dissolve the sugar, until small bubbles form around the edge.

Meanwhile, in a mixing bowl, whisk the remaining ¾ cup of cold milk into the cornstarch. Whisk in the egg yolks. Slowly stir in ½ cup of the hot cream mixture, then slowly stir this mixture into the remaining hot cream. Cook, continuing to stir, about half a minute more until the mixture forms soft shapes when dropped from a spoon.

Remove the custard from the heat and stir in the vanilla. Transfer to a medium-size bowl and stir occasionally to allow steam to escape. Stir in all but ¼ cup of the coconut. Cover the surface with wax paper or plastic wrap to prevent a skin from forming and cool for 1 hour at room temperature.

Preheat the oven to 350°F.

In another bowl, beat the egg whites until soft peaks form. Slowly beat in the sugar and cream of tartar and continue to beat until the meringue is shiny and holds stiff peaks.

Spoon the cooled custard into the prebaked pie shell and spread the meringue over the pie, covering the entire surface. Sprinkle with the remaining coconut. Bake on the center rack of the oven until the peaks are golden, about 10 minutes. Let cool and refrigerate for 1 hour before serving.

Serves 8 to 10

NO-BAKE REFRIGERATOR CHEESECAKE PIE

This is a quick and easy, lowfat version of a no-bake cheesecake. There is no cream cheese or egg in the recipe. It is not as rich as a New York–style cheesecake, but it is very satisfying to your sweet tooth. It freezes for 3 months.

2 tablespoons (¼ stick) butter, melted
¾ cup graham cracker crumbs
2 envelopes unflavored gelatin
½ cup cold water
½ cup lowfat milk
2 cups lowfat cottage cheese, drained
½ cup lowfat Yogurt Cheese (page 19)
1 cup sugar

1 teaspoon vanilla extract
2 tablespoons grated lemon peel (no white attached)
¼ cup lemon juice

GARNISH
Blueberries, strawberries, or other fruit (optional)

Combine the melted butter and the graham cracker crumbs. Press the crumbs firmly onto the sides and bottom of a 9-inch pie pan. Refrigerate for at least 30 minutes.

In a small saucepan, sprinkle the gelatin over the cold water and let stand 3 minutes. Heat on very low heat until the gelatin has dissolved. Pour the milk and the dissolved gelatin liquid into the bowl of a food processor and process for about 10 seconds. Add the drained cottage cheese, Yogurt Cheese, sugar, vanilla, lemon peel, and lemon juice and puree until smooth and creamy, about 20 seconds. Pour the mixture into the prepared pan and refrigerate for about 6 hours, or until set. Cut into wedges with a sharp knife that has been warmed in hot water. Serve garnished with fresh fruit or berries if desired.

Serves 8

SWEET POTATO PECAN PIE

Steve and Rodney Farmer, my apprentices, developed this recipe for our pantry Thanksgiving. Canned sweet potatoes may be substituted for the cooked potatoes. If you like sweet potatoes, you'll *love* this. It has the texture of a sweet potato pie with a pecan pie on top. The baked pie can be frozen for up to 3 months.

CONVERTING DEEP-DISH PIE RECIPES
If you do not have a deep-dish pie pan, make the pie as directed in the shallower pan, and bake the remaining filling in a greased custard cup. Reduce the cooking time by one-third and check every 5 minutes until done.

1¼ pounds sweet potatoes (about 2 large)

½ cup (1 stick) butter, melted

¾ cup packed dark brown sugar

2 large eggs, at room temperature, lightly beaten

1 teaspoon grated lemon peel (no white attached)

¼ cup heavy cream

¼ teaspoon salt

TOPPING

¾ cup granulated sugar

¾ cup dark corn syrup

2 large eggs, lightly beaten

1½ tablespoons butter, melted

2 teaspoons vanilla extract

Pinch of salt

Pinch of ground cinnamon

¾ cup pecan halves

1 deep-dish piecrust, partially prebaked (page 197)

Preheat the oven to 450°F.

Bake the potatoes directly on the oven rack until they are soft, about 45 minutes to 1 hour, depending on the size of the potatoes. Reduce the temperature to 350°F. Cool slightly, then split the potatoes and scoop the soft insides into a bowl. Add the butter, brown sugar, eggs, lemon peel, cream, and salt and beat briefly with a whisk or mixer just until smooth and well blended.

For the topping, combine the sugar, corn syrup, eggs, butter, vanilla, salt, and cinnamon in a medium-size bowl and stir them together with a wooden spoon. Stir in the pecans.

Spoon the sweet potato filling into the pie shell, smooth the top, and spread the topping over it. Cover the edge of the crust with aluminum foil. Bake the pie in the center of the oven until it puffs and sets and is a deep gold, about 45 minutes to 1 hour. Remove from the oven and carefully remove the foil. Cool on a rack and serve warm.

Serves 8 to 10

CARAMEL BROWN SUGAR PIE

For brown sugar addicts, this pie is a godsend. It's a pure, unadulterated down–home tribute to its title. It's a very fast filling—ideal to accompany fresh fruit or berries if you have them. It doesn't take much people time—it just bakes on its own. And best of all, you've got all the ingredients right on your shelf.

HOW TO FLUTE A PIE CRUST
There are many ways to decorate the rim of a pie crust. The easiest is to crimp it by making a "v" with the thumb and index finger of one hand. Pinch a bit of the rim in the "v" and then press the crust into the "v" with the index finger of the other hand. Move a "v" length away on the rim and repeat until top rim of the pie is uniformly crimped.

2 recipes Lu Len's Beginner's Piecrust (page 197) or 2 frozen piecrusts

FILLING
¼ cup (½ stick) butter, at room temperature
6 tablespoons all-purpose flour

½ cup heavy cream
2 cups firmly packed brown sugar, light or brown according to your taste
2 eggs, lightly beaten
2 teaspoons vanilla extract
1 cup fresh or frozen or defrosted berries or peaches, for garnish (optional)

Preheat the oven to 375°F. Line an 8–inch pie pan with one of the defrosted crusts or half of the pie dough. Roll out the remaining dough or crust into a round to top the pie.

Stir the butter with the flour in a heavy saucepan over low heat to make a smooth paste. Whisk in the cream and sugar. Bring to the boil, reduce the heat, and simmer the filling until it thickens, about 3 minutes, whisking constantly. Add a small portion of the warm liquid to the eggs, then stir them into the pan. Stir in the vanilla. Strain the filling into the lined pie pan.

Top with the round of pie dough and crimp the edge decoratively to seal. Cut 4 to 5 slits in the top to allow steam to escape. Bake until the crust is nicely browned and the filling is set, 45 minutes to 1 hour.

Serve with the fresh berries or peaches if using.

Makes 1 8-inch pie

LU LEN'S BEGINNER'S PIECRUST

This is the best shortening piecrust I know. You can use butter or margarine for some or all of the shortening if you prefer. So one way or the other you'll have everything you need on hand. You can roll it out enough for a deep-dish pie or double it for 2 crusts. Lu Len developed this recipe when she lived with me while in school eight years ago and I still love it—and miss her!

1½ cups all-purpose flour
½ teaspoon salt

½ cup shortening
4 to 8 tablespoons ice water

Mix the flour and salt together in a bowl. Cut in the shortening with a pastry blender or fork until the shortening is the size of green peas. Loosely separate the flour-fat mixture, still in the bowl, into 3 portions. Add ice water, a little at a time, to 1 portion, tossing the mixture with the pastry blender or fork until it is moist and holds together. Set that section aside. Repeat with the other portions. When all the portions are moistened, gather them into a ball and flatten into a round disk. Wrap in plastic and chill ½ hour or more.

Flour a board or wax paper and, using a floured or stockinged rolling pin, roll the pastry into a round about ⅛ inch thick and at least 1½ to 2 inches larger than your pan. Fold in quarters. Place the pastry in a 9-inch pie pan and unfold. Trim the pastry 1 inch larger than the pie pan and tuck the overhanging pastry under itself. Then use the thumb and index finger of one hand and the index finger of the other to flute the edges. Place in the freezer or chill in the refrigerator for 30 minutes before baking.

To prebake, preheat the oven to 400°F. Crumple a piece of wax paper, then spread it out to the edges of the pan. To make a weight, fill the paper with raw rice or dried peas. Bake for 20 minutes. Carefully remove the paper and rice or peas. (The rice or peas may be used again the next time you prebake a piecrust.) Fill the crust with a filling and bake according to the filling directions. If the filling requires no cooking, bake the pie shell 10 minutes more.

Makes 1 9-inch pie shell

SWEET DOUBLE PIECRUST

This flaky piecrust can be used for most sweet pies or tarts. Divide in half for a single-crust pie and freeze the other half for a rainy day.

2½ cups all-purpose or soft-wheat flour
¾ teaspoon salt
2 tablespoons sugar

½ cup solid vegetable shortening
½ cup (1 stick) butter
6 to 9 tablespoons ice water

Sift the flour, salt, and sugar together in a bowl. Cut in the shortening and butter with a pastry blender or fork until the mixture resembles peas. Add the ice water, a little at a time, tossing the mixture with the pastry blender or fork until the dough is moist and holds together. Gather the dough into a ball, divide it into 2 pieces, and flatten each into a round. Wrap each piece in plastic and refrigerate for at least ½ hour, or longer if possible.

Flour a board or wax paper. Using a floured or stockinged rolling pin, roll 1 pastry round out ⅛ inch thick or less and at least 1½ to 2 inches larger than your pan. Fold the round in quarters, place it in a 9-inch pie pan, and unfold it. Trim the pastry 1 inch larger than the pie pan. Chill 30 minutes.

After filling the bottom crust, roll out the second piece the same way and place on top of the filled pie shell. Fold the overhanging pastry under the bottom crust, then either press the tines of a fork around the edge to form a pattern or use your 2 thumbs to flute the dough all around. Cut decorative slits in the top crust and bake according to your recipe.

Makes 1 9-inch double piecrust or 2 9-inch single crusts

THE DAIRY CASE

If you have milk (or cream), cheese, and eggs, you can have a variety of meals. Butter helps, too. There are omelets, soufflés, overnight puddings made with bread and eggs (stratas), quiches, baked custards, meringues, crème anglaise and other boiled custards, hollandaises, béarnaises, mayonnaises, and a host of other recipes.

It's important to remember that many variables affect the life of a dairy product—whether it's covered or wrapped, the type of container, storage temperature, etc. Many, such as the ultrapasteurized creams, have shelf lives of over a month, however, and are worth keeping on hand. (They can be diluted with water to substitute for milk or used as is for decadent coffee, cereal, etc. Once opened, most last only a week!) Remove only the portion of the dairy product to be used and return the remainder to the refrigerator.

Generally, a dairy product will remain fresh and usable for a few days beyond its pull date or sell-by date. Regulations vary among states.

Here are some general guidelines:

Serve milk cold and store in the refrigerator after opening. Use proper containers to store at refrigerated temperatures (40°F.) or below as soon as possible after purchase.

Keep milk containers closed to prevent absorption of other food flavors in the refrigerator. An absorbed flavor alters the taste but the milk is still safe.

Keep canned milk in a cool, dry place. Once opened, it should be transferred to a clean opaque container and refrigerated.

Milk can be frozen for up to twelve months if stored at −10°F., but it won't be popular to drink or on cereal as it usually separates. I usually only freeze it when I know otherwise it will be bad by the time I use it, and then use it only for emergency cooking.

Evaporated Milk

Canned evaporated milk is made by evaporating enough water from whole milk under vacuum to reduce the volume by half.

Powdered (Dry) Milk or Buttermilk

Store powdered milk or buttermilk in a cool, dry place and reseal the container after opening. Humidity may cause lumping and affect flavor and color. If such changes occur, the milk should be used immediately. Substitute reconstituted milk or buttermilk freely for fresh in baking or cooking; it should be covered and stored in the refrigerator as you would any other milk.

Sweetened Condensed Milk

Sweetened condensed milk is a canned milk concentrate of whole or skim milk with a sweetener added. It is not a substitute for evaporated milk.

UHT Milk or Cream

UHT or Ultrahigh temperature milk is processed in a similar way to ultra-pasteurized milk and cream, but it is packaged in sterilized containers. It can be stored without refrigeration up to three months. It seems to be more popular in Europe and England, where I first used it, than in the United States. Once opened, it should be refrigerated.

Heavy and Whipping Cream

Cream can be frozen, as evidenced by the successful use of frozen cream by the ice cream industry. However, particles of fat are evident when frozen cream thaws. Generally, home freezing of cream produces an unsatisfactory product. Similarly, sour cream does not freeze well, although some dishes prepared with sour cream can be frozen without adverse effects. Heavy cream is 36% fat, whipping cream 30%, by law.

Whipped cream can be satisfactorily piped into rosettes or other shapes onto a flat baking sheet. When frozen, place individually in a tightly covered storage container and freeze until needed. Try to serve frozen. They usually won't weep.

Butter

Butter freezes well for about three months. It is best removed from its carton and rewrapped in freezer wrap or a freezer bag. I admit to freezing it in its box, however, and have not always been unhappy with the results. I prefer using salted butter if I am to keep butter in the refrigerator for more than three days, as I find unsalted takes on some flavors from the refrigerator. I keep unsalted well wrapped in the freezer for baking or omit extra salt from baking if salted is all I have. I leave my butter out of the refrigerator in a covered butter dish whenever possible, as I love soft butter on my bread. I think I use less when it is at room temperature than when it is hard to cut. Margarine may of course be substituted if you like, and it does keep well in the refrigerator or freezer.

Cheese

Cheese should be refrigerated at temperatures between 35°F. and 40°F. in its original wrapper or a container, tightly wrapped in foil or plastic wrap to protect it from drying out. Cheese with a strong aroma, such as Limburger, should be stored separately in a container with a tight-fitting lid to prevent the odor from being absorbed by other foods. For best flavor and aroma, serve cheese, except for fresh cheese such as cream, cottage, and Neufchâtel, at room temperature.

No matter how carefully natural cheese is stored, it will continue to ripen and will eventually spoil. Generally the harder the cheese, the less moisture it contains and the longer it will keep. In country stores you see it kept at room temperature under a glass lid. Very hard cheeses such as Parmesan will keep in the refrigerator several months; they freeze well. cheddar and Swiss have slightly more moisture and will keep several weeks in the refrigerator. I freeze them for cooking. Fresh and soft cheeses such as cottage and ricotta contain the most moisture and thus are the most perishable. They should be eaten within one week of purchase. I freeze them for cooking. Cream cheese has a longer refrigerator life and can also be frozen.

Mold may occasionally develop on the surface of natural cheese. Although most molds are harmless, some may produce toxins that could penetrate the cheese. To be safe, cut away one-half inch of cheese on all sides of visible mold. Use the remaining cheese (I hope there is some left!) as quickly as possible.

Most hard cheeses can be frozen, but freezing will cause changes in texture. For this reason, thawed cheese is best used shredded or crumbled in salads, as a topping, or in cooked dishes. For best results:

1. Freeze pieces of ½ pound or less.
2. Use moisture-proof and airtight wrapping.
3. Freeze quickly and store at 0°F. no longer than three months.
4. Thaw, wrapped, in the refrigerator.
5. Use as soon as possible after thawing.

The following cooking equivalents can be used for measuring:

1 cup shredded cheese = 4 ounces cheese
1 cup crumbled cheese (such as blue) = 4 ounces cheese
1 cup grated hard cheese (such as Parmesan) = 3 ounces cheese

Eggs

Refrigerated, they will keep several months, although the grocery store pull date is usually less. Discard any eggs that may be cracked. Eggs can also be kept on the shelf for some time—my grandmother kept them for months—even though they shrink and taste funny and must be thoroughly cooked, which is a good idea whenever you cook eggs, especially if they'll be eaten by anyone very young, elderly, or ill.

BIBLIOGRAPHY

Bailey, Lee. *Tomatoes*. New York: Clarkson N. Potter, Inc., 1992.

Beranbaum, Rose Levy. *Rose's Christmas Cookies*. New York: William Morrow, 1990.

Betty Crocker's Cookbook. New York: Golden Press, 1969.

Carrier, Robert. *Great Dishes of the World*. London: Thomas Nelson and Sons, Ltd., 1963.

Clayton, Bernard. *Bernard Clayton's New Complete Book of Breads*. New York: Simon and Schuster, Inc., 1987.

Eckhardt, Linda W. *Bread in Half the Time*. New York: Crown Publishers, Inc., 1991.

Emory University Woman's Club. *Emory Seasons*. Memphis, TN: Wimmer Brothers, 1993.

Goodbody, Mary, and editors of *Chocolatier Magazine*. *Glorious Chocolate*. New York: Simon and Schuster, Inc., 1989.

Green, Jane, and Choate, Judith. *The Gift Giver's Cookbook*. New York: Simon and Schuster, Inc., 1971.

Greene, Bert. *Greene on Grains*. New York: Workman Publishing, 1984.

Haedrich, Ken. *Home for the Holidays: Festive Baking with Whole Grains*. New York: Bantam, 1992.

Haughton, Natalie Hartanov. *Cookies*. Tucson: HP Books, 1983.

Hayes, Joanne Lamb, and Leblang, Bonnie Tandy. *365 Great Cookies and Brownies*. New York: HarperCollins Publishers, 1993.

Hazan, Giuliano. *The Classic Pasta Cookbook*. New York: Dorling Kindersley, 1993.

Hazan, Marcella. *The Essentials of Classic Italian Cooking*. New York: Alfred A. Knopf, 1992.

Herbst, Sharon Tyler. *Food Lover's Companion*. New York: Barron's, 1990.

Kurzweil, Raymond. *The 10% Solution for a Healthy Life*. New York: Crown Publishers, Inc., 1993.

Lee, Karen, with Branyon, Alexandra. *Nouvelle Chinese Cooking*. New York: Macmillan Publishing Co., 1987.

McCune, Kelly. *The Art of Grilling*. New York: Harper & Row, 1990.

Merinoff, Linda. *Gingerbread*. New York: A Fireside Book, 1989.

Mitchell, Paulette. *15 Minute Vegetarian Gourmet*. New York: Macmillan Publishing Co., 1987.

Netzer, Corinne. *101 Low Cholesterol Recipes*. New York: Dell Publishing, 1993.

Ojakangas, Beatrice A. *Pot Pies. Forty Savory Suppers*. New York: Clarkson N. Potter, Inc., 1993.

Olney, Judith. *Judith Olney on Bread*. New York: Crown Publishers, Inc., 1985.

The Red Star Centennial Bread Sampler Milwaukee, WI: Universal Foods Corp., 1981.

Root, Waverly. *The Cooking of Italy*. Alexandria, VA: Time-Life Books, 1978.

Rosenberg, Judy. *No-Holds-Barred Baking Book*. New York: Workman Publishing, 1991.

Russo, Julie, and Lukins, Sheila. *The Silver Palate Cookbook*. New York: Workman Publishing, 1979.

Sahni, Julie. *Classic Indian Cooking*. New York: William Morrow, 1980.

Schloss, Andrew, with Bookman, Ken. *Fifty Ways to Cook Most Everything*. New York: Simon and Schuster, Inc., 1992.

Schulz, Phillip Stephen. *Cooking with Fire and Smoke*. New York: Simon and Schuster, Inc., 1986.

Senior, Dorrit Speyer, and Payne, Rolce. *Cooking with Fruit*. New York: Crown Publishers, Inc., 1992.

Spry, Constance, and Hume, Rosemary. *The Constance Spry Cookbook*. London: J. M. Dent and Sons, Ltd., 1967.

Su Jan, Lee. *The Fine Art of Chinese Cooking*. New York: Gramercy Publishing Co.

Tung, Pat. *Pat Tung's Cooking School*. New York: Simon and Schuster, Inc., 1985.

Wolfert, Paula. *The Cooking of the Eastern Mediterranean*. New York: HarperCollins Publishers, 1994.

INDEX

EQUIVALENT IMPERIAL AND METRIC MEASUREMENTS

American cooks use standard containers, the 8-ounce cup and a tablespoon that takes exactly 16 level fillings to fill that cup level. Measuring by cup makes it very difficult to give weight equivalents, as a cup of densely packed butter will weigh considerably more than a cup of flour. The easiest way therefore to deal with cup measurements in recipes is to take the amount by volume rather than by weight. Thus the equation reads:

1 cup = 240 ml = 8 fl. oz.   ½ cup = 120 ml = 4 fl. oz.

It is possible to buy a set of American cup measures in major stores around the world.

In the States, butter is often measured in sticks. One stick is the equivalent of 8 tablespoons. One tablespoon of butter is therefore the equivalent to ½ ounce/15 grams.

Liquid Measures

Fluid ounces	U.S.	Imperial	Milliliters
	1 teaspoon	1 teaspoon	5
¼	2 teaspoon	1 dessert spoon	7
½	1 tablespoon	1 tablespoon	15
1	2 tablespoon	2 tablespoon	28
2	¼ cup	4 tablespoon	56
4	½ cup or ¼ pint		110
5		¼ pint or 1 gill	140
6	¾ cup		170
8	1 cup or ½ pint		225
9			250, ¼ liter
10	1¼ cups	½ pint	280
12	1½ cups	¾ pint	340
15	¾ pint		420
16	2 cups or 1 pint		450
18	2¼ cups		500, ½ liter
20	2½ cups	1 pint	560
24	3 cups		675
			or 1½ pints
25		1¼ pints	700
27	3½ cups		750
30	3¾ cups	1½ pints	840
32	4 cups or 2 pints or 1 quart		900
35		1¾ pints	980
36	4½ cups		1000, 1 liter
40	5 cups or 2½ pints	2 pints or 1 quart	1120
48	6 cups or 3 pints		1350
50		2½ pints	1400
60	7½ cups	3 pints	1680
64	8 cups or 4 pints or 2 quarts		1800
72	9 cups		2000, 2 liters

Solid Measures

U.S. and Imperial Measures		Metric Measures	
ounces	pounds	grams	kilos
1		28	
2		56	
3 ½		100	
4	¼	112	
5		140	
6		168	
8	½	225	
9		250	¼
12	¾	340	
16	1	450	
18		500	½
20	1¼	560	
24	1½	675	
27		750	¾
28	1¾	780	
32	2	900	
36	2¼	1000	1
40	2½	1100	
48	3	1350	
54		1500	1½
64	4	1800	
72	4½	2000	2
80	5	2250	2¼
90		2500	2½
100	6	2800	2¾

Oven Temperature Equivalents

Fahrenheit	Celsius	Gas Mark	Description
225	110	¼	Cool
250	130	½	
275	140	1	Very Slow
300	150	2	
325	170	3	Slow
350	180	4	Moderate
375	190	5	
400	200	6	Moderately Hot
425	220	7	Fairly Hot
450	230	8	Hot
475	240	9	Very Hot
500	250	10	Extremely Hot

Linear and Area Measures

1 inch	2.54 centimeters
1 foot	0.3048 meters
1 square inch	6.4516 square centimeters
1 square foot	929.03 square centimeters